DATE DUE

MAY 23 '02			

HIGHSMITH 45-220

books by Ruby Berkley Goodwin

IT'S GOOD TO BE BLACK

A GOLD STAR MOTHER SPEAKS

FROM MY KITCHEN WINDOW

TWELVE NEGRO SPIRITUALS
by William Grant Still, stories by
Ruby Berkley Goodwin

it's good to be black

RUBY BERKLEY GOODWIN

SOUTHERN ILLINOIS UNIVERSITY PRESS

Carbondale and Edwardsville

Feffer & Simons, Inc.

London and Amsterdam

to mother

whose valuable assistance made the
writing of this book a pleasure and
a sacred trust.

**ARCT
URUS
BOOKS** ®

Copyright, 1953, by Ruby Berkley Goodwin
All rights reserved
Reprinted by special arrangement with the heirs
of Ruby Berkley Goodwin
Preface by Carmen Kenya Wadley, copyright © 1976
by Southern Illinois University Press
This edition printed by offset lithography
in the United States of America

Library of Congress Cataloging in Publication Data

Goodwin, Ruby Berkley.
  It's good to be black.

  (Arcturus paperbacks; AB133)
  Reprint of the 1954 ed. published by Doubleday,
Garden City, N.Y.
  Autobiographical.
  1. Goodwin, Ruby Berkley. I. Title.
[E185.97.G64A3   1976]   301.45'19'6073024 [B]
ISBN 0–8093–0757–X   53–11462

BY CARMEN KENYA WADLEY
Granddaughter of Ruby Berkley Goodwin

Preface

Is it good to be black? To Ruby Berkley Goodwin it was. What did she see in being black that made her call it "good" long before "black is beautiful" became a popular slogan? How did she manage to find goodness and pride in being black before naturals (afro hairdos) and black history classes became fashionable? This book was first published in 1953; at that time, the civil rights movement, Martin Luther King, Jr., Malcolm X, and the Black Panthers were either relatively unknown or they did not exist. During this time, most American blacks referred to themselves as "colored" or "Negro"; to be called "black" was as bad as being called a "nigger." Why did she believe that black was good? The black that she writes about has nothing to do with skin color, but it does have a great deal to do with self images, values, spiritual strength, and most of all love. Unlike the contradicting definitions of blackness we see reflected in today's crime statistics, movies, television, newspapers, political speeches, advertisements, and sociological and psychological reports; Ruby Berkley Goodwin's definition of blackness is simple and to the point, black is good. "It's Good to be Black" is more than the story (history) of a black family living in Du Quoin, Illinois, during the early 1900s; it is a reaffirmation for all of us who know in our hearts that there is still good in the world and that some of that good is black.

October 1974

foreword

Until I once argued with a psychology teacher, I didn't know that all Negro children grow up with a sense of frustration and insecurity. Moreover, I still feel that this statement, along with such kindred observations as "all colored people can sing and dance," must be taken with the proverbial grain of salt.

The philosophy behind this remark, however, I have since found implied in most books about Negroes. Whether the authors are black or white, they are equally guilty of representing us either as objects of pity or as objects of contempt, and I have learned to resent this implication much as I earlier resented the flat remark of the psychology teacher.

As a result I have felt impelled to write of life as I have lived it. I sincerely believe the lives of many Negro children follow the same pattern as did mine. We have probably been overlooked by writers because it is much easier to dramatize the brutal and the sordid than the commonplace.

I am not so naïve that I wish to imply being black is a bed of roses. Life is a serious business whether one is white or black, but in our town there were few penalties that could be traced directly to color.

We were fortunate in having Braxton and Sophia Berkley for parents. What couldn't be soothed by Mother's calm assurance was always solved by Dad's positive action. To us he was a combination of Einstein, Flash Gordon,

Sherlock Holmes and Santa Claus. There wasn't anything he wanted to do that he couldn't do. Moving a mountain? Why Dad had only to lean his little finger against it to send it flying over into Jackson County.

My frustrations based on color did not come in childhood. They came with maturity, after I had left my father's house—after we had pulled up our roots and left the friendly little town of Du Quoin.

A child's sense of security and his normal pleasures depend for the most part on the wisdom of the adults with whom he lives. This observation lay behind the writing of this book.

While we were going over the unfinished manuscript one day, these thoughts were crystallized in my mind by a remark made by my dear friend, the late Dr. Karl Downs. "Ruby," he commented, "to be born black is more than to be persecuted; it is to be privileged."

contents

1. Du Quoin, Illinois — 13

2. as a fruitful vine — 22

3. Cousin Frankie — 33

4. the black man's strength — 43

5. before our time — 50

6. Sunday morning — 62

7. we become a race of champions — 71

8. when the black spider crawled — 80

9. we witness a hanging — 88

10. and may the best man win — 96

11. carnival time — 110

12. echoes of Algiers — 124

13. I've never seen "Uncle Tom's Cabin" — 140

14. the stranger within our gates — 148

15. we attend a baptizing — 161

16. strike! — 167

17. miracle on Smoke Row 181

18. balancing the score 187

19. living is fun 193

20. a bishop visits our city 203

21. Davis' mine goes on a rampage 213

22. Dad converts a socialist—almost 223

23. our pioneers in race relations 228

24. the ugly mask of fear 237

25. black and powerful 246

it's good to be black

1. Du Quoin, Illinois

The little town of Du Quoin sat in the heart of the coal belt of southern Illinois. It was as though the officials of the Illinois Central Railroad had placed a dot along the tracks between Centralia and Carbondale and said, "Let's put a town about here." But such was not the case, for Du Quoin had pulled stakes and of its own accord shifted ten miles to the east to spread itself along both sides of the tracks, even though a few stubborn souls who resented change stayed in what we called Old Town, with its crossroads general store, small-steepled church, and burying plot.

The Du Quoin I knew was a frisky, healthy upstart of a town, yet there were weeks of saneness when life was as flat and stolid as the vast prairie upon whose bosom it rested. Its tempo was heightened when there was an explosion at the mines, or when the quick flash of a stiletto left a body lying in a pool of its own blood on a street corner in Little Italy. General elections, medicine men, the Ringling Brothers Circus, Buffalo Bill and his Wild West Shows were talked about long after the brilliant-colored posters had become indistinct patches of paper against the barns where they had been posted.

Only the uninitiated spoke of Du Quoin as a whole. The town was divided by invisible but well-defined lines. The natives called the various sections the Bottoms, Smoke Row,

13

Little Italy, the North End, Cairo, the East Side, and Little Egypt.

Du Quoin was a place of old faces and familiar scenes. There were no dirty company houses ready to fall apart at the first gust of north wind. The miners, for the most part, owned the little four- and five-room L-shaped cottages where they lived by the will of the operators, who regulated the days of work by the rise and fall of the coal market in New York. The operators in their two-story mansions, set among box hedges and rose gardens, lived by the sweat and brawn of the miners, though they never openly conceded this point.

We lived in the Bottoms, in one of these little cottages at the extreme end of South Walnut Street. Dad was a coal miner. He had come up through the hard school of experience from a green "trapper" to one of the best entry drivers in southern Illinois.

He was the eldest son of an ex-slave, but because mining coal was a hard and dangerous job, no one was too concerned about a miner's background. If he knew his business he was accepted as a fellow worker, and that was his admittance card into the great fraternity of free men.

When I look back on my childhood, I am conscious again of the security that comes from growing up in one neighborhood, knowing everybody in town, living almost two decades in the same house, and being surrounded by the same people. I realize that there could be a tiresome monotony to this type of living, but I cannot conceive of boredom with Braxton and Sophia Berkley for parents, or Helen, Spud, Cecil, Robert, Cliff, Tom, and Frances for brothers and sisters.

Life in Du Quoin wasn't for the timid or pampered. The

14

men who crawled about underground, by the faint glare of a carbide light fastened onto their caps, by-passed death a hundred times during the day as they adjusted props to hold up roofs of hanging coal, side-stepped a slide, or eluded the well-aimed hoof of a vicious mule.

The strength of the women matched the fiber of the men as they worked in their homes, cared for their many children, boiled their white clothes in a zinc tub over an open fire in the yard, and hustled the oldest boy off to Frank Knight's saloon for a cool bucket of beer at noon.

When there was an explosion at White Ash mines, the colored people weren't too bothered. They talked about it, to be sure, but all agreed that God was venting his wrath upon the operators who never permitted Negroes to work there. Their summarization of the disaster was, "God sho' don' love ugly."

But if something went wrong at Old Enterprise, Horn's, Eaton's, or the Majestic, the whole populace hurried on foot down the dusty roads that led to the mines. Neighbors who hadn't spoken for years suddenly became friends as they milled around, tense and trembling until every man was accounted for—dead or alive. In the terrible waiting someone would mutter, "Devil sho' is busy." Thus every happening was speedily rationalized as being either the work of the Lord or the trickery of the devil.

While the mines were our chief interest the gashouse also came in for a share of youthful concern. There red-eyed Simon fired the brick furnaces that gave lighting to the street lamps and the homes of the wealthier townspeople. Sometimes we would stop to watch him shovel coal into the blazing mouths. When he had finished, he would wipe the perspiration from his face with a large red and white bandana, then with head thrown back he would read the gauge to the left of the door. Simon could not write and somehow we got the impression that he could not read the gauge. Often we predicted that one day Simon was going to have one beer too many, get up too much heat, and blow up the gasworks. This never happened, much to our disgust. We learned early why most prophets are without honor.

Leaving the gashouse, by cutting across the vacant lot next to John and Rosa Rapuzzi's house, one came out on South Walnut Street, just a half block from our house. Walnut Street was wide and unpaved. The trees were not uniform as to size or species, for the four small maples in front of our house were dwarfed by the tall poplars that shaded Aunt Belle's front porch across the street. Our house hugged the ground. Because the wind could not get beneath it during a blizzard, all the neighbors came over and sat with us while their houses rocked and shuddered at the mercy of a terrific wind. Nellie Wilburn's house in the next block was also used as a storm cellar when the wind storms came, but next to it pigeon-toed Lettie Clary's house caused us much anxiety. The ground had an uncomfortable way of opening up during the night and sinking sometimes three or four feet at the northwest corner of the house. The neighbors would hurry over with their supply of empty cans and bottles and when the hole was filled, Luther and Ural, Lettie's sons, would level it off with dirt. This had to be done once or twice every year. Dad said the Clary house had been built over a worked-out mine. We expected some morning to wake up and find a gaping hole with no trace of the Clarys or their house. But like the explosion at the gasworks, this never happened either.

Money in a mining town is made to spend; any bartender, peddler, merchant, or fancy woman will tell you that. Du Quoin was blessed, or cursed, according to your point of view, with plenty of saloons, and endless streams of peddlers, and a representative number of sporting houses.

The "red-light district" had no well-defined boundaries. The colored prostitutes could be found on North Oak and South Division streets. Two or three doors north of Lettie Clary's house the white district began. When it reached the corner it fanned out in both directions on Franklin Street while it continued its crimson path into the next block on Walnut. On the west side of the street it stopped at Julie Jackson's unpainted house. Then came Uncle Joe Dement's house, set well back in a spacious yard overrun with trees and rambler roses. On the other side of the street the houses of assignation stopped next door to Wade and Mary Ramsey's cottage, which sat opposite Jake Druer's palatial residence. No one thought it strange that one of the town's successful white businessmen lived for years in front of a very ordinary Negro family on the fringe of red-light district. This was the west side of Du Quoin at its democratic best.

The red-light district was one of those taken-for-granted things, and one thought little about the painted Magdalenes who stood on their front porches and openly solicited trade. They were the only women who ever smoked in public. Part of their stock in trade were sheer stockings and silk underwear. The decent women confined themselves to thin nainsook lingerie and lisle hose.

Passing through this district on our way home, we soon knew all the girls' lines of approach. If the weather was warm, Nellie sat demurely on the porch reading a book. In the winter she sat by the window; the lace curtains, carefully drawn back, formed an artistic background for her fragile pink and white beauty. She never looked up, no matter if a regiment marched by. Tommie stood in the front door. Her smile was as warm as a June morning. "Hi there, Shorty," or "Come on in, Slim," or "Whadda ya say, Red?" were her set phrases. We knew them all by name and always spoke when we passed. It was considered good manners to speak to everybody in Du Quoin.

Sometimes at night innocent women were accosted if they had to go through the district to reach their homes. This fact often formed the basis for a reform plank in a candidate's election platform. Several times Helen and I were the "innocent women," as we sprinted through the district with some out-of-town white Lothario at our heels. We soon learned to duck into Lettie Clary's yard yelling, "Open the door, Mama." The man, who may have been color-blind, or who may have heard from some unreliable source that even unwilling colored girls gave more inspired sexual performances than willing white ones, would turn quickly on his heels and disappear up the street.

The red-light district was no more glamorous to us than Bradley's cooperage where they made barrels. Indeed the cooperage was more intriguing, for as Frog Larson knocked the staves together, he sang the blues. We never saw the words written down, but we learned them by heart as we stopped on our way from school and leaned in the window while Frog worked and sang:

> Some say high yaller,
> Some say high yaller,
> But I say give me black or brown, babe;

> Some say high yaller,
> I say give me black or brown;
> Black gal won't leave you,
> Brownskin won't turn you down.
>
> Muddy wada risin'
> Muddy wada risin'
> Muddy wada risin' 'round mah head, Lawd;
> Muddy wada risin'
> Wada risin' 'round mah head;
> Tired o' muddy wada
> Almos' wish that I was dead.

Frog sang with his mouth full of nails. There was perfect co-ordination as his tongue pushed the nails forward. Machine-like, the thumb and forefinger of the left hand grasped the nail just below the head and held it securely against the staves while the claw-toothed hammer in his right hand pounded it into place.

One block farther, Walnut crossed Main Street. Here began the business section of Du Quoin. On the southwest corner was Charlie Florence's saloon. As the doors swung back and forth you could see men sitting about drinking beer. Card games were going on at some of the tables. A long bar stretched the length of the south wall. Over the long sectional mirror at the back of the bar, several daring pictures of girls peeping coyly from behind fans and large hats showed well-shaped limbs with sheer hosiery, topped by a pair of lace-trimmed garters just above the knees.

Directly across the street stood the large red brick Catholic church and the parochial school. Schleper's grocery store stood on the northeast corner. From the southeast corner, Henry Stoutenberg's shoe repair shop looked diagonally at Father Clockie and the somber-clothed nuns, and face-tiously sported these words beneath his cobbler's sign, "We also take care of your soles."

Looking east on Main Street, names as familiar to us as our own were painted on the glass windows or above the store fronts—Henry Fritz's Meat Market; W. W. Parks, Drugs and Sundries; Joe Lipe's Saloon; John Simmon's Poolroom; the Du Quoin Bank of Henry Horn; and the old mill that completely hid the Illinois Central depot. Arthur Angel's drugstore was on the corner of Main and Division streets. Half a block north was Forester's company store. Most of us could have gone there blindfolded.

Practical Du Quoin made one concession to culture. That is the only possible explanation for the Majestic Opera House, with its plush seats, its ornately scrolled boxes, and its marble foyer. *Uncle Tom's Cabin* and *The Georgia Minstrels* were billed annually. *Madame X* and *Within the Law* were great favorites. One year John Phillip Sousa brought his band to the Majestic. Salem Tutt and Tutt Whitney treated Du Quoin to the highest-class colored entertainment it had ever seen when they brought their show, *The Smarter Set*, for a three-night run.

We used the whole of the East Side as a park for promenading. When the weather was good, little intimate bands from the west side would go walking, sometimes as far as the cemetery at the extreme northeast end of the town. We walked leisurely, each choosing the house that suited his or her fancy. The streets were wide and shaded with large oak and sycamore trees. These were the homes of the Popes, the Musselmans, the Brookings, the Butler Halls, the Pyles, and Arthur Angel.

The west side could boast of homes of equal grandeur,

but they were the exceptions and not the rule. The homes of Frank Schleper, W. W. Parks, Judge Wheatley, and Frank Wells surpassed many of the East Side homes, but we lived with these people as neighbors and so were not awed by their dwelling places.

People have a tendency to absorb into their personalities the spirit of the land upon which they live. Tragic events were like the infrequent electric storms of August or the blizzards in February and March. They shook and frightened the town, it is true, but the roots of the people were planted too deeply to be disturbed by even the most horrible incident.

The broad prairies, stretching out on every side of the town, gave one a sense of the continuation of the beautiful and good. The maple, birch, and poplar trees made a jagged line on the western horizon. Quiet creeks and streams that never ran dry suddenly found themselves part of the great Mississippi River that rose to appalling heights every spring, climbing over man-made dikes, washing the lowlands, and sending the people of Mounds City and Cairo to shelter on higher ground. Farmers worked the brown clay earth with well-fed, plodding dray horses. A fine thread of coal dust from the tipple houses told of men crawling about beneath the earth mining the coal to keep homes warm and the factory wheels turning.

This was Du Quoin. Something in its nature reminded you of a two-faced woman. It could be as friendly as a Maltese kitten; then it could be a great little town for minding its own business. . . .

2. *as a fruitful vine*

The ever new miracle of birth was an old, old taken-for-
granted thing in the Berkley household. For the fourteenth
time in her twenty-three years of married life, Mother was
going down into what was often referred to as "the valley
of the shadow."

The first four boys, true to a gypsy's prediction, had died
at birth. "There'll be no luck for you till the sex changes,"
the woman had prophesied as she shook her head sadly.
The golden earrings and the brightly colored scarf swayed
ever so gently as she turned away, too impressed by the
tragedy she had seen in Mother's hand to ask for a piece
of palm-crossing silver.

Helen was born next, a little saffron cherub with a head
as bald as a teacup, smiling almost from the moment she
caught her first frightening breath. Dad and Mother never
got over the wonderment of her victorious clinging to life.
My advent was less novel, and by the time Braxton Junior
(whom we called Spud), Cecil, Roggie, Lester and Robert
came along, squalling long-headed, bow-legged babies were
an old story. How Mother and Dad managed to maintain
an air of joyful expectancy as we put in our appearance
every two years, come hail, hell, or high water, I have never
been able to discover.

World happenings were catalogued in the Bottoms by the
birth of Mother's youngsters. Cliff was born just before a

young student assassinated an archduke and his wife in far away Bosnia. Tom came shortly after we entered the first World War. The armistice had been signed and the guns were now silent. The boys in khaki were returning home from the battlefields of Europe, and the people in the Bottoms awaited the birth of Sophia's new baby.

Usually Dad was the first one up to start the fires, but not so on Christmas morning. Even before daybreak, curiosity had chased the sleep from our eyes. A whispered "See anything?" came from near the bedroom door. I answered back a negative "uh-uh!" Spud crept to the center of the room near the base-burner. I slid out of bed. Together we tiptoed about the room. Helen slept soundly as did the smaller children in the next room.

Through the semi-darkness we could see long-ribbed cotton stockings, knotted with Oregon apples and Florida oranges, hanging about on the walls, like stumpy chicken snakes full of eggs. A small table near the south wall held cereal bowls of Christmas candy shaped like bows and rosettes. There were chocolate drops and creamy white sticks with intricate colored designs running through the center. Pecans, almonds, Brazil and English walnuts were mixed with the hickory nuts and scaly-barks we had gathered in the fall on the banks of Big Muddy Creek.

Spud shook down the ashes and soon had a roaring fire in the base-burner. The younger children were now awake, and as they crowded about the pile of gaily wrapped presents on the floor they glanced impatiently toward the bedroom where Mother lay. Dad hushed their inquiries with a simple statement, "Your mother don't feel so well this morning." Immediately, we became silent and unconsciously grouped ourselves in the bedroom door. We had forgotten the presents and the Christmas goodies in our anxiety.

Whether Aunt Dea was sent for or just happened to drop in, we never knew. Somehow she was there, nudging toys and young ones gently aside with her foot, sashaying into the bedroom with a steaming cup of tea, and stuffing a twenty-pound turkey Mother's brother Sargeant had sent her from California. Under her clipped commands and searching eyes the folding bed in the living room became a davenport, ashes were brushed from the faded floral rug, chairs were pushed against the walls, lamps were filled, and chimneys were polished. The pungent smell of celery, onions, garlic, and sage filled the four rooms and slipped quietly outside where it hung about the porches in the crisp December air.

It was early afternoon when Aunt Dea, after numerous trips into Mother's room, came back into the kitchen and sent Helen and me to call Dr. Gillis.

"Hit the grit!" she ordered. "And don't stop to talk." With Aunt Dea, a doctor was the last resort. This may have been due to the heavy strain of Indian blood that fought for domination over her Negroid heritage. She was tall and angular, and so marked were her Indian features that a band of Cherokees who once came to town with Buffalo Bill followed her home, grunting gibberish to her all the way. We knew her trusted remedies, sugar and turpentine for stomach-ache or cramps, onion syrup for coughs, jimson weeds dampened and tied on the forehead for headache, and red pepper and corn meal poultices for pneumonia. When Aunt Dea didn't trust these, the patient was mighty sick.

We pulled on our fleece-lined overshoes, buttoned our

heavy coats about our throats, and tied woolen fascinators under our chins.

Dr. Gillis and sickness were synonymous, and the former usually arrived just a jump or so behind the latter. Even if the bony finger of death had rapped on the window and beckoned for you to follow, Dr. Gillis had only to poke his shiny head in the door to send the grim monster packing.

As Helen and I hurried along, I thought of a remark Dad had made. "He's something like the Lord. Any time you call Dr. Gillis, he'll come." We ran every step of the way, the deep snow clinging and pulling us back as we lifted our feet from the heavy drifts. We were out of breath when we reached the gashouse where the only phone in our part of town hung in a smoky little aperture on the wall. Coming from the dazzling whiteness outside, the interior of the plant was dismal. The red glow from the open door of the furnace cast an eerie light over the half-bent solitary figure at the other end of the building.

"Can we use your phone, Simon?" I called.

Simon, slim, black, and perspiring in spite of the zero weather outside, stopped scooping the shovelsful of nut coal, mopped his brow with a large bandana, and answered, "Sho, sho. How's Mis' Sophia?"

"She ain't so good. Aunt Dea sent us to call Dr. Gillis." Even as I answered Simon I was turning the crank and listening for the voice of the operator. Simon's eyes took on the glare of the furnace as he stood within the circle of its light, resting himself on the handle of the shovel.

Despite the frequency of childbirth in our household, we had never associated anything painful or unpleasant with it. Mother was a Spartan, and there was never an outcry or a moan. As we grew older however, we became apprehensive for we remembered Mrs. McLemore, who never walked another step after Lora was born. Then there was the young wife, Lilly Rivers, who never lived to see her baby. Her cries of pain were choked by the death rattle in her throat.

Dr. Gillis' voice boomed at me through the receiver, and suddenly the words I wanted to say knotted in my throat. Helen looked at me anxiously, her small round face catching the edge of my own terror. "Hello, hello," said the impatient voice. I'm going to fail Mother, I thought. I'm going to stand here like a rock and Dr. Gillis is going to hang up, and a terrible darkness will sweep over the counterpane with Mother's face showing over the edge of it.

Then, miraculously, the urgency came rising up in me and I was answering Dr. Gillis with a thin, quavering voice.

"This is Ruby Berkley, Dr. Gillis. It's Mama's time," I kept saying, "It's Mama's time." I was still holding the cold black instrument in my hand after Dr. Gillis had finished his mutterings about a kettle of fish, plenty of hot water, and coming as soon as he could get there.

We lifted our feet high as we walked across the vacant corner lot, pausing to catch our breath and look at the familiar landscape. The dwellings of the miners and the pretentious homes of the operators and merchants were softened by the snow that blanketed the town with its ermine whiteness. Rimmed by the broad acres of farm land, the tipple houses above the mines were not unlike slender church spires.

Dad had evidently been watching, for as we started around the house the front door opened and he called to us. His face, the color of unpolished old bronze, was filled with apprehension. When he knew that Dr. Gillis was on his way, some of the lines disappeared. He smiled a little, showing strong, even mother-of-pearl teeth. With his right hand he absent-mindedly stroked the heavy mustache that almost hid his upper lip.

Mother's bed which was usually flush against the east wall had been pulled out. Aunt Dea was busy smoothing out several thicknesses of a worn sheet blanket beneath her. A red velvet motto, "God Bless Our Home," hung by a silk cord on the wall above the bed.

Mother's smile was wan and detached. I asked her if I could get something for her. She shook her head, and for the first time I noticed the small beads of perspiration that stood out on her forehead. The heavy reversible spread she had bought from an Italian peddler was carefully folded back and made a colorful strip across the foot of the bed. Her hands gripped the nine-patch quilt of gingham blocks that lay across her full breast.

"Don't be botherin' yore ma with foolish questions. Git!" Aunt Dea started us from the room with a wave of her hand. As I turned to go, I noticed a pair of scissors someone had carelessly left on the bed. I reached back and picked them up, this time addressing my question to Aunt Dea. "You don't need these, do you?"

She looked up again. Her brown hand dropped the fold of the blanket and darted through the air like the hooded head of a cobra. She snatched the scissors from me fiercely and pushed them under the spread. "Leave 'em be," she hissed. "Something sharp on the bed—anything sharp—will help cut the birthing pains."

Back in the kitchen I picked up a paper-bound copy of *St. Elmo*, the then current best seller. The moody hero and pious Edna Earl were far from my mind. I put the book aside and went to the north window where Helen sat watching a group of boys playing snowballs. She had almost forgotten the matinee party she had been invited to and the dinner to follow at the farmhouse of Mr. Vincent, the only colored farmer who lived east of town. Those exciting, red-letter events had been pushed gently aside that morning by Dad's quiet understatement that Mother didn't feel well. Helen turned around addressing no one in particular. "Here's Dr. Gillis."

Aunt Dea came to the window, took one look and shouted, "What in God's world is the matter with Dr. Gillis?" To us, there was nothing strange about his actions. He was patting Cecil on the head, then carefully giving him the small black bag he had pulled from the seat of his car. Now he was striding up the cinder-strewn walk with Spud and Cecil on either side of him. Robert and the other boys were still standing by the car, some watching the trio as they advanced toward the house, others making faces at themselves in the shiny fenders or gliding their hands over the large convex headlights.

Aunt Dea, with a woman's eye for detail, had noticed the satin stripe down the trouser legs. Thin wisps of sandy hair peeked from beneath a high top hat. Instead of the practical Scotch-plaid muffler he usually wore, a most dressy silk-brocaded scarf was looped over and tucked beneath the lapels of his heavy black broadcloth topcoat.

At the door, Cecil gave the bag back to Dr. Gillis and he and Spud turned to rejoin their comrades. Dr. Gillis greeted us all by name as he entered the house. Both Aunt Dea and Dad towered over the short Scotch-Irishman. He walked into the bedroom and over to Mother's bed and smiled down at her as he reached back to give Aunt Dea his topcoat, scarf and hat. Then Helen and I noticed for the first time his formal cutaway coat, the white vest and the pleated stiff-bosom shirt with the pearl studs down the front. Aunt Dea was about to burst wide open with curiosity, but she said nothing as she folded the coat and scarf and carefully laid them on the boys' bed in the next room. She put the top hat on the dresser. A hat on the bed was bad luck and Aunt Dea was taking no chances. Mama needed all the good luck we could muster up for her. When Tom, who now toddled about the floor, was born, Dr. Gillis had told Mother and Dad there should be no more children. Aunt Dea and Aunt Ida had been saying that for years but Mother and Dad had paid them no mind.

Just as most children carry on the deception of a belief in Santa Claus for the benefit of their parents, so it was with our knowledge of birth. We had never been told the fascinating story of the birds and the bees. The extent of our sex education had been the rather casual admonition at about the age of thirteen to "keep your dress down." Nevertheless, we knew that germinating a new life was due to some sort of strange and mysterious rite legally reserved for married folks.

Activities in the bedroom seemed to speed up. Dr. Gillis had replaced the cutaway coat with his white surgeon's smock. Aunt Dea had put a few drops of a queer-smelling disinfectant in a basin of warm water and had held it while he washed his hands. The copper kettle on the back of the stove had been kept filled with boiling water. The steam had long since chased the frost from the windows.

Aunt Dea was kept busy between the kitchen and Mother's room. She tore ragged sheets, saved especially for this occasion, with a great ripping noise, and muttered to herself about the unfairness of a providence that made good women suffer while no-'count men got off scot-free. From time to time she basted the Christmas turkey, put out vegetables for us to prepare, or sent us on errands up to Aunt Ida's house.

Everyone in the neighborhood knew that Mother's time had come. Kate Seaman, a little German lady who lived directly north of us, came over with a steaming bowl of soup, "to giff 'er strent." But Mother was too busy for eating, and shortly after the door had closed behind Kate, a breathless, terrifying wail sounded through the house.

The crying stopped almost as quickly as it had begun. There were sounds of quick movements, clipped monosyllables, breathless silences. Then came the voice of Dr. Gillis weighted with good-natured scolding and intense relief. "Young lady," Dr. Gillis held the small bundle in his arms, "you sure played hell with Du Quoin society this afternoon. I'm supposed to be playing best man to Harry Miller and here I am tying your navel cord."

"Helen, it's a girl." I was slightly disappointed with Mother.

"Well, I'm glad. I'm tired of old long-headed boys." There had been seven boys in a row.

Presently, Aunt Dea came to the door and beckoned with her index finger. "Dr. Gillis said you could see your little sister now."

We went into the room. Dad was leaning over the bed, looking at something almost hidden in a downy pink and white blanket. He and Dr. Gillis were smiling as though they were well pleased with themselves. Mother's smile was different. It was weak but relaxed. Her eyes were tired but shining. I wanted to lean over and kiss her but I was shy,

as a fruitful vine

and contented myself with a peek at the baby before Helen nudged me out of the way so that she could get a better look.

The new baby was named Frances Ann for her two grandmothers. Dr. Gillis wrote the name on a small pad, returned the pad to his pocket and slid into a cane-bottom rocker.

"Sophia, I know you did all the work, but I'll be damned if I'm not tired, too." He rested his elbow on the arm of the chair and covered his eyes with his hand. When he addressed Dad, he spoke softly as though speaking more to himself. "Braxton, you've got a fine family."

"I think so too, Doc. 'Course it's a poor dog that won't wag his own tail."

After a few minutes, Dr. Gillis stood and moved slowly about the room. He fitted the small vials and bottles into his bag, then pulled on his gloves. Dad held his topcoat. "How much is the bill, Doc?"

Dad reached in his pocket and handed Dr. Gillis two bills. "I'll catch up the slack in the next couple of paydays," he promised.

"Don't worry about me, Braxton. You've got too many mouths to feed. I'm not trying to get rich off of you. And don't think I'm sympathizing either. You're a millionaire." A thread of envy could be traced in Dr. Gillis's voice, for he and his wife were childless.

If Dad sensed the wistfulness he ignored it by saying, "Wish I could make 'em believe that millionaire stuff up at the company store when we're out on strike."

Dr. Gillis had reached the front door. He adjusted his silk hat and stepped out upon the porch. The snow on the walk had been packed hard by the tramping of many feet.

Christmas, always a day of delightful surprises, had out-done itself. Along with Roman Beauty apples, peppermint sticks, toys and dresses, it had brought us an olive-tinted baby, whose advent had delayed Du Quoin's most fashion-able wedding for two whole hours.

3. *Cousin Frankie*

I was never overawed by accounts of the pyramids of Egypt or the leaning tower of Pisa. Cousin Frankie was the first wonder of my childhood world. Between us was an invisible yet vibrant bond of appreciation and understanding that is seldom found except between the very old and the very young. My spirit, still encased in a dream world of its own making, met and blended with hers that had been softened and refined in the furnace of fiery trials.

Cousin Frankie was blind as a mole—had been blind for twenty years. She did not walk with the halting uncertain step of the sightless. Her step was firm. She carried her head high. Her eyes were not dull or cloudy. They were alive and sparkling and seemed to be looking straight at you. The Illinois Central Railroad that divided the town, rode a man-made rise behind her house. She could go all over the neighborhood alone, except when the snow covered the worn footpaths that gave her direction.

My most enjoyable chore was leading Cousin Frankie about the shaded, unpaved streets of Du Quoin. We were a familiar sight—a spindle-legged slip of a girl with large brown eyes set in a sallow brown face, and an old blind woman. Cousin Frankie was well-cushioned and of medium height. Her nose was flat, yet slightly bulbous. Her mouth was large and unsmiling. Her white frizzly hair was usually covered by a calico dust cap that matched the basque she wore, and her dust-catching black woolen skirt was splotched with streaks of green from long wear. The swish of her full stiff petticoats played a soft accompaniment as we strutted jauntily through the streets.

Every Wednesday evening we went to prayer meeting at Mt. Olive Baptist Church. There, with a few other devout souls, she would meet for a long season of prayer, thanking God for his many blessings and praying for an uncaring world that was "leapfroggin' right into the middle o' hell."

Cousin Frankie was an ardent worshipper. Unlike Zacharias who was struck dumb as he served at the altar, Cousin Frankie's words flowed like molten lava. She made her supplications knee-bent and body-bowed, but with a pleasing oratory that, according to Elder Winston, "could move the throne of God."

Saturday was an equally pleasant day. Bright and early we went shopping. Cousin Frankie would lay in a week's supply of staples, Garrett snuff, and gumdrops. The latter she shared with every child who came to her house.

Nobody had ever given me lessons on leading blind people. Her hand rested lightly on my arm and only when she was unsure of herself would the gnarled fingers tighten their grip. She matched her step with mine and the few directions I had to give were very simple. When we came to a curb I said, only loud enough for her to hear, "Step down." Almost across the road a "Step up" would lift her to the sidewalk without losing our pace.

Cousin Frankie lived with her sister, Nettie. They were as unlike as two sisters could be. Nettie was a thin wisp of a woman and the sharp features of her cocoa brown face were set in a perpetual smile. Nettie worked out nearly every day, so Cousin Frankie did the housekeeping that kept their home immaculate. Her thorough sweeping soon wore all the nap off the rugs. She took in a few bundles of laundry, could iron simple pieces, and make plain garments like aprons and chemise. She spent most of the day alone and her husky contralto voice was often lifted in song:

> What you gonna do wi' the motherless chillun?
> What you gonna do wi' the motherless chillun?
> What you gonna do wi' the motherless chillun,
> In-a that lan', 'way ovah there?
>
> Gonna take 'em in mah ahams an' care 'em to Jesus,
> Gonna take 'em in mah ahams an' care 'em to Jesus,
> Gonna take 'em in mah ahams an' care 'em to Jesus,
> In-a that lan', 'way ovah there.

Nettie didn't seem to worry about leaving her alone during the day. Her chief concern was getting Cousin Frankie off her knees at night. She prayed night and morning, kneeling by her old oval-topped trunk behind her bedroom door. She prayed for everybody and it took her some time to cover all the ground, especially when she even remembered the kings and princes in the foreign countries. Sometimes old Satan sneaked up and threw sleep powder in her eyes. A snore would give her away. Poking her head into the bedroom, Cousin Nettie would shriek impatiently, "For God's sake, Frankie, get up from there before you take the gallopin' consumption on that cole floor."

Everybody in the neighborhood considered it a privilege to help Cousin Frankie. If she wanted to start supper before Cousin Nettie came home, there was always a volunteer to wash her greens or put the ham hock in the heavy iron pot. We were our sister's keeper. That is, almost always. Sometimes when there was a good show at the Lyric and Spud didn't have quite enough pennies, some of Cousin Frankie's dish towels, which she usually hung on the grape arbor, would find their way into his rag bag.

Old Man Dellums, the insurance man, was the exception. He collected fifteen cents every week on Cousin Frankie's burial policy. Sometimes he failed to mark the correct number of weeks paid and sometimes he shortchanged her. He couldn't fool her on buffalo nickels; she knew their feel. But sometimes he passed the other kind off for quarters and whenever we saw him coming down the street, clutching his premium book under his arm, one of us would saunter across to her house.

Early in life, misfortune had made Cousin Frankie's bed. Married to Mose Robinson, a colorful singer and preacher, he had deserted her shortly after the birth and death of her first baby. Like the legendary John Henry, Mose had a "run-around on his foot and women on his weary mind." Even the rival elders conceded that "Mose could preach the devil outa hell." When he stood in the pulpit, eyes closed, his big body swaying as he crooned "Jesus Gonna Make Up Yore Dyin' Bed," every woman in the church felt that it would be all right if only Mose Robinson was there to cradle her head on his broad chest.

Each time Mose left, Cousin Frankie would swear that she would never take him back, didn't want to see him again, didn't want to talk about him. She sang a great deal but the joy songs she started always changed to sorrow songs. Then one day Mose would walk up the narrow footpath and the icy shield Frankie had placed before her heart would chip and crumble beneath the warmth of his smile and the fire of his full lips. Frankie would lie contentedly in his arms trying hard not to think of the other women who had been held and fondled by this same Mose Robinson.

She refused to listen to her heart which told her that one day the going would be for good. She missed looking up to see Mose's giant form filling the doorframe and for a moment blotting out the light. She missed his booming voice and the tremulous rattle of window panes as his songs vibrated throughout the house. She missed the stirring of the little life beneath her heart. Her arms ached and her breasts tingled for the soft pull of tiny puckered lips. The hours moved more slowly than giant crawfish climbing slowly up the side of a steep pail, falling back, and starting the climb to nowhere again.

In view of all this, it was only natural that as soon as Dr. Gillis was out of the house I scampered across the road to tell Cousin Frankie and her sister Nettie about our Christmas baby. Nettie dozed by the small heater in the sitting room. I did not disturb her but passed into the kitchen where Cousin Frankie was washing dishes. She dried her hands quickly and tossed the dish towel over a thin line behind the cookstove. Snatching her worsted cape from the back of the chair in the room where Cousin Nettie nodded, Cousin Frankie reached the door before I did.

We started out, but before she closed the door Cousin Frankie looked back and called, "Nettie, Nettie." Cousin Nettie didn't open her eyes, but grunted "huh?" through closed lips.

"I'm goin' over to see Sophie's new baby." Cousin Frankie did not stop to find out whether Cousin Nettie caught the meaning of her words. We were off the porch and our feet were making crunching noises as we broke the thin icy surface that had formed above the soft snow.

Aunt Dea met us at the door. Taking Cousin Frankie's cape, she hung it on the back of the chair, all the time inquiring about her state of health, asking after Cousin Nettie and informing Cousin Frankie of a new pain in her ankle that so far had resisted the potency of White Mountain liniment. Dad walked through the house boastful, useless, and proud. Helen, who was setting the table, stopped in her counting of plates to mumble her greeting.

We were always forgetting that Cousin Frankie could not see; so Aunt Dea nodded her head towards the door Dad had just disappeared through and said, "Sophie's in there."

Cousin Frankie seemed to know what she meant for there was no question in her voice as she replied, "I'll warm up a bit before I go in. May want to hole the li'l mite." She stretched her fingers toward the base-burner as she inched nearer its warmth.

"Spec this 'bout winds up Sophie's row o' chile bearin'," were her first words of general conversation. "When the first young'un was born, me an' Aunt Milly White counted fourteen knots on the navel cord. You can always tell how many babies a woman gonna have, if you know what to look for. I could see then," she hastened to add.

Aunt Dea grunted assent about knowing what to look for, but she was still dubious about Frances Ann being the last baby. "I hope you're right," she muttered as she pushed the cane-bottom chair closer to Cousin Frankie. "Keep trying to tell Braxton and Sophie the Lord didn't put 'em here to populate the world by themselves."

Cousin Frankie

Dad was no stranger to Cousin Frankie; so she chuckled softly to herself as she answered, "Spec you was tole to go on 'bout yore nee-mind."

"Braxton talked a lot of fool talk about the Bible sayin' be fruitful an' multiply. He ain't learned that 'rithmatic got a take-away sign too."

"Ole robber death plays wid dat sign." Cousin Frankie's voice was low, yet a fear had crept into it—a fear and a hatred too. We were all quiet as we thought of Roggie and Lester, our two little brothers, who had stopped by our house for a brief bright moment before the take-away sign had been put in front of their names. In the silence I could hear her voice saying, "I could see then."

It wasn't long after the birth of Mother's first baby that Cousin Frankie knew something was happening to her eyes. At first, she thought the days were murky. As objects grew more indistinct, she realized with shocking clearness that she was going blind. Soon she would no longer be able to watch the maple leaves cover the ground like a gorgeous Persian rug each fall. There would be no more delightful excursions into the woods to gather wild mustard in the spring. She would not be able to sit on the banks of Big Muddy Creek and watch her cork bob upon the water before a wily cat-fish jerked it underneath.

"I could see then." There was proudness and pathos in the deep husky voice. Entwined with the wistfulness were strong threads of gratitude for the precious possession of sight that most of us accept as casually as we take a three-cent stamp from the smudgy fingers of a postal clerk. As I watched her I was again filled with wonder at her patience, kindness, and at the trace of the mystic that made her seemingly casual statements words of prophecy.

Aunt Dea's voice brought me back to the immediate present. "Sophia had easy labor this time."

"Tha's good." Cousin Frankie nodded her head.

"I made her walk as long as she could stand up," Aunt Dea continued. "Then when she laid down I rubbed her back. Sophia says the onliest time in her life when her back hurts is when she's havin' a baby. Well, I done everything I could remember. Sure gave Sophia a good workin' over. It was the easiest birth Sophia ever had. That young'un like to got here before Dr. Gillis."

They laughed and I smiled to myself as I remembered the time I had shocked Aunt Dea with the simple statement that Mama was going to have a baby. That was just before Cliff was born and, of course, I was much younger.

Aunt Dea had bristled, "Oh, so your mother has babies, eh, Granny?" She had looked over the glasses that rode the bridge of her beak-like nose. Disapproval sat on her face like the topknot on a Houdan hen. Helen had wanted to laugh but knew better.

"Yes," I began. Helen was shaking her head furiously. I wanted to tell Aunt Dea that as soon as Mother pulled off her nicely fitted gingham dresses and started wearing the flowered calico wrappers that Rosetta Froner made her, we knew she was going to have a baby. But old people are so hard to teach anything, my eleven-year-old mind reasoned then; so if Aunt Dea, who was an old maid, wanted to believe that Dr. Gillis was going to bring the baby, well, it wouldn't hurt her.

Cousin Frankie was warm by now and asked to be taken into Mother's room. Her full lips broke into one of her rare smiles, "Well, Sophia, ole lonesome valley done los' its terror."

"Yes, Cousin Frankie."

"An' this soon you done forgot the feelin' of the pain." Her voice was warm with understanding. She held out her arms and there was the ring of a command in her voice as she asked permission to hold the baby.

Dad, who was sitting by the bed, rose and fumbled with the folds of the blanket. With a "let me," Aunt Dea pushed him aside and carefully placed Frances Ann in Cousin Frankie's outstretched arms. There was a hungry possessiveness as she gathered the little form to her bosom. There was an extra brightness in the sightless eyes. Just as Dr. Gillis' voice had unconsciously told of his secret longing for a child of his own, Cousin Frankie's eyes spoke of rivers of unshed tears.

For a few seconds her coffee-colored face rubbed the fleecy blanket. Her body rocked to and fro as though the strains of a lullaby had been tuned in to her ears alone. Now she stood perfectly still, her head raised in an attitude of listening. She did not have to tell us what she was doing. We knew. Instantly our eyes closed and every head was bowed. The place where we were standing had become holy ground.

"Good afternoon, Jesus. This is ole blind Frankie. I ain't much, but I'm here to talk to you." We saw a spirit humbled by circumstance, mellowed by tribulations, bowing low before the throne of God.

"First, Lawd, we want to thank ya that when we rose this mornin', our bed was not our coolin' board, nor our cover our windin' sheet. Kind Jesus, we'se comin' to you in the humbles' manner we knows how, askin' yore blessin' on this new soul you done gone an' brung into this sin-tryin' worl'."

Despite the humility, Cousin Frankie prayed as one having authority. "She's a stranger to us, Lawd, but she ain't no stranger to you. You knowed her before the foundation of the world. Mah Lawd, you knowed her even before there ever was a when or a where, a then or a there, a go-out-yonder, or a come-back-here. Give her wisdom, Lawd, an' understandin'——"

"Yes, Jesus," burst from Aunt Dea's lips.

A shaft of late afternoon sun caught Cousin Frankie and the baby in a prism of soft liquid gold.

"An' grace to run wid patience the race that is set before her," she continued. "Guide this tender little soul through this wilderness of howlin' wolves an' temptin' devils. Keep her outa the gunshot of ole Satan, an' when it comes ours to swap time fo' eternity, bear us over Jordan where we can praise yore name forever. Amen!"

4. *the black man's strength*

The clanging of the fire bell jarred the stillness that lay over our town just before daybreak. Whether I was awakened by this or Dad's exclamation of "Great God a' mighty!," I do not know. Dad was looking out of the north window, his flannelette nightshirt striking the calves of his legs.

Mother called from her bedroom, "What's on fire, Braxton?"

"Can't say. A fire's deceiving. May be the old Schleper place—then again, "there was a slight pause, "may be farther north."

Mother seemed reluctant to suggest, "The church?"

Dad was back in the bedroom trying to assure Mother that it couldn't possibly be the church. His voice was muffled as though he were pulling something over his head. Now the assurance had changed to inquiry and anxiety and I could catch such words as "but the baby is still too young —this cold night air" caught and held between Mother's insistence that she "felt fine" and "Frieda Molsen," a Polish woman in the next block, "met Dr. Gillis at the front door the very next day after her baby was born."

From the sounds I knew they were dressing hurriedly. Soon they were passing through the living room where Helen and I slept on a folding bed. Dad was turning up the collar of his overcoat. Mother was throwing the ends of her fascinator around her neck.

43

Just as they reached the door I started to question them. Then I quickly reasoned if I said nothing there would be no stay-at-home orders; so I lay quiet until they passed out of the door.

They had not reached the sidewalk before I was out of bed and at the window. The whole north end of town was a huge bonfire. Spiraling fingers of red and orange lost themselves in the billowing smoke clouds that hung suspended above the glow. I ran into the room where the boys were sleeping and shook Spud vigorously. I did not wish to disturb the others; so I whispered, "Wake up, Spud. Wake up." I had no fear of waking Helen. She was a sound sleeper, and I only hoped that Gabriel's lung power would be sufficient to blast her awake on Judgment Day.

The shaking brought nothing from Spud but a few grunts. He turned to his side and mumbled, "Knuckle down." I pounded his shoulder and was finally rewarded by the opening of one eye, glazed with sleep.

"There's a big fire, Spud. Wake up," I pleaded, "Wake up." The first eye was closed again, but the other was slowly opening. "You fudged," Spud pouted. Finally he sat up in bed, still groggy but slowly beginning to comprehend. His first intelligent comment was, "Let's go."

We were now at the north window, eyes wide, mouths open. Soon we were fully dressed and were half running, half sliding up the icy streets.

The south end of town lay in the soft shadows of a premature sunrise. Hatted and hooded figures called muffled greetings to one another as they came out of their yards. The whole town was awake and on its way to the fire.

When we reached the red brick Catholic church we could see the Schleper house standing intact, its two stories outlined by the fire that burned fiercely farther north. Mother had been right. It was the church. It was Grandpa Holmes' church. No, it was not Grandpa Holmes' church. Sure he had given up his salary while they were building to make it easier on his congregation. Sure he had climbed about, lifting his heavy body by his strong arms and shoulders, for Grandpa Holmes had only one leg. Sure he had carried the dream of that church in his heart for many years. The Lord had sent the vision to him one night and he saw the finished edifice, complete to bell tower and baptismal pool. The great bell had come all the way from Akron, Ohio, and even L. K. Williams, the biggest Baptist preacher in the state, had left his church in Chicago to come and preach the dedication services. Black and white ministers had sat side by side on the rostrum and talked warmly of the faith and patience of Elijah Holmes who had built this magnificent temple unto the Lord.

But Grandpa Holmes had never taken the credit. He had helped, yes. But there had been so many hands. There were the saffron hands of his second wife, Cordelia, who went from door to door selling extracts and cheap perfumes and spices to help feed them as Elijah lifted and pulled the heavy beams into place. There were the coffee-bean brown hands of his eldest son John who painted portraits of the fashionable and rich at his studio in St. Louis, whose hands had coaxed exquisite music from the deep-toned organ of an exclusive white church. John had drawn the plans under his father's supervision. There were the coffee-and-cream brown hands of Aunt Tolitha, Aunt Judith, and Mother, their younger sister, who with the other women had cooked innumerable meals for the crowds of men, German, Italian, Irish, Swedish, Polish, and other uncatalogued white Amer-

45

icans who had joined the Negro workers at the church when the mines were idle. There were the small eager hands of young boys who had carried numberless pails of water to the thirsty men as they sweated in the hot sun. There were the hands of others who trudged over the East Side holding miniature churches with slits in their steeples for "anything you can afford to give us."

This was the people's church and that was the way Grandpa Holmes had wanted it. For the God he served was not exclusive. He was God of all. And now this temple that had been dedicated three short months ago was wrapped in flames. The town stood silently by and braced itself against the temporary rope barrier put up by the firemen who now tugged at the slippery hose and played the small streams of water over the holocaust.

Freeman Sampson stood holding the little cast iron bell he had used to call the Sunday school to order. It was the only thing he had snatched from the heavy oak table when he had dashed into the burning building to be driven back by the searing flames.

Tobe Thomas, Aunt Tolitha's husband, had reached for a David C. Cook Sunday School chart as he was forced back outside by the heat and the cries of the early arrivals who called, "you can't save nothing—get outa there!" He had not thought to roll it up and lay it to one side. He walked about through the crowd muttering and shaking his head, unmindful of the glaring picture of the shepherd boy David with his small slingshot, hurling a defiant challenge to the giant Goliath.

We did not seek Mother and Dad out, but it seemed everywhere we looked they were there and we knew it would not be long before they would want to know, "Who told you to come up here!" Aunt Emma Harris, Miz Cordelia's mother, recognized no one. She stood watching the fire as though fascinated. But as we watched carefully we saw her lips moving in prayer and passing close by we heard her groan "Merciful Jesus!"

The hunk of tobacco in Cy Kelly's right jaw made him look like he had the toothache. He rolled it around furiously, and finally expelled it contemptuously from his mouth. The veins in his forehead stood out and there was a spasmodic throbbing at the temples. "The son of a bitch that started this oughta be throwed right in the middle of it," he finally exploded.

Dad who was standing nearby answered him, "Elder Holmes would be the last man to agree with you."

A voice that I did not recognize agreed with Cy Kelly. "You can be too good."

"I ain't saying that's the way I feel. I ain't a preacher. I know the Good Book says to turn the other cheek, but if a son of a—a gun hit me he sure better be gone when I turn the other cheek," Dad commented.

"You're damned right," Cy nodded his head. His short, bitter laughter was lost among the crackling of the flames and the falling of burning timber.

We found Grandpa Holmes and Miz Cordelia across the street, over on Lew Smith's porch. Lew Smith ran a saloon but he and Grandpa Holmes were good friends. Someone had pulled a chair out on the porch for Miz Cordelia and she sat hunched over, rocking to and fro as great sobs tore and wrenched her frail body and tears squeezed themselves through the fingers that covered her eyes.

Grandpa stood looking towards the church, but one hand rested tenderly on the shoulder of the woman who had worked with him to make the vision appear real to all men.

"Don't carry on so, Cordelia. This is not the end. We're all together," and he looked down to where Gilbert and Emery crouched close to their mother. "It was just a building of wood and stone and glass. We built that—we can build another." There was no life in his voice as on the day when we stood with him and watched the sun streaming through the stained glass window above the altar. "I have builded a house unto the Lord," he had said with simple, humble pride. The gold threads that formed the cross on the black altar cloth were soft and warm, and Grandpa's uplifted face wore the satisfied look of a man who after years of hard labor gazed with affection on the fruition of his dream.

"We can build another," Grandpa had said, but we knew this was not so; and strangely enough we knew that he knew we knew. But as we looked up at his face we did not see the heavy tracery of defeat. There was a sadness, a great sadness. There was resignation as though he knew, with a certainty past all doubting, the will of his God, and had already said a silent yes to the power that had permitted this strange and awful thing to happen.

I felt a tear on my cheek and quickly lowered my head and brushed it aside with the back of my hand. I looked at Grandpa Holmes again. This time I was struck by the quality of strength I saw there. There was still the quiet resignation, but there was also the strength of a stout willow, to bend in the storm without breaking. It was a strength for burden bearing. A strength to wait through the long night for a morning that promised nothing. Some of this strength must have oozed from his finger tips into the frail shoulders of Miz Cordelia. She was quiet now, and they both looked across to the ruins of the church. The flames had burned themselves out and the constant play of water sizzled and sputtered over the dying coals.

Thus, in the early morning hours as we turned away from the red cinders that blackened even as we looked at them, there was born in me a great respect for the black man's strength.

His is the strength of the beaver and the ant. The strength of the tireless little people of the world to build and rebuild. Patience and the ability to make a dream grow in the barren soil of nothingness—this is the black man's strength, sometimes seemingly powerless but always magnificent and—indestructible.

5. *before our time*

The Genicio yard was one of the show places in Du Quoin.
One of the houses in the first block of Little Italy, it was a
place of beauty and wonderment. Firello Genicio, lured to
America from his native Italy by dreams of a fuller life in
a new world, had built a miniature Italian village in his
frontyard.

Whenever Mother sent me on an errand to her older
sister, Aunt Tolitha, I always passed that way. Today I was
doing the very commonplace thing of taking a gallon of
freshly churned buttermilk out to Aunt Tolitha's. Young
Tony Genicio was sitting on his front porch.

As I slackened my pace, Tony looked up and spoke to me.
His greeting was friendly but casual.

"I always come this way." I hung over the fence, looking
at the little village with its spired cathedral and its narrow
streets. "It's the most beautiful thing I've ever seen."

"It's the village where my dad lived." Tony slid from the
porch and came over to the fence. "Dad says that's just the
way it is. Here's the house where he was born. There's the
church where he was baptized. It's all there."

"Gee. It must be wonderful to be able to do that. Is your
dad an artist?"

Tony laughed at my ignorance. "Dad an artist? Hell, no.
He's just a coal miner."

"Well he could be——"

"You mean he could have been if he had stayed in the old country. Wait, let me show you——" Tony hurried into the house and was soon back with a framed picture. It was a cathedral intricately designed with arches and spires and statues. "This his grandfather designed. He was the great one. Maybe if Dad had stayed in Italy——"

As I walked on toward Aunt Tolitha's house I found Tony's innocent disclosure very disturbing. He had not shown me the cathedral to be bragging. He had simply responded to my appreciation of his father's work. Tony's great-grandfather had designed a cathedral. What had my great-grandfather done? The question plagued me. I should find out.

Somehow during the course of small talk I asked Aunt Tolitha. She threw back her head and laughed. "How should I know—guess he was running around in a g-string somewhere."

The answer didn't satisfy me. I hurried home and asked mother the same question. She looked at me strangely as though trying to fathom what was behind the question. She started to ask me a question but seemed to think better of it.

"I'm glad you asked. Sometimes we don't talk much about our ancestry. We're too close to slavery and that's something we try to forget. It's not a pretty story, but it's a brave story. I've heard Mother Berkley speak of it so much I know it as well as I know my own family history."

Dad's people had come to Du Quoin from Island Number 10 shortly after the close of the Civil War. Island Number 10 was a small island in the Mississippi River near the Illinois line, where runaway slaves were kept in protective custody by the Union government to prevent slave traders and former owners from taking them back south.

Dad came from a family of nonconformists. His grand-mother, Judy, had definite ideas about love and marriage which didn't quite fit into the pattern of selective breeding used on some southern plantations.

To escape the attentions of a healthy young buck who had been picked by her master to mate with her, Judy per-formed a few commando tactics on the young man, slipped away from the plantation before daybreak and made herself comfortable in an Alabama swamp.

For three years she lived there alone. The only people she saw were the few brave slaves who slipped into the swamp after dark to bring bits of food to keep her from starving. Sometimes they would try to persuade her to come back to the plantation.

" 'Taint safe, Judy. 'Taint safe for a lone 'oman."

"In-a da daytime Ah make frens wid da animals. Ain't nothin' wild effen you kin ta'k hits own ta'k. De night ain't bad nuther, caise Ah allers knowed how to ta'k wid Jesus, but in de swamps Ah done learnt to let Jesus ta'k to me. We done come ta be de bes' o' frens," Judy answered them.

Being defied by a young girl was not good for the morale of the plantation. Finally John Hopgood called the slaves together in the big yard. They were apprehensive and fright-ened. They talked under their breath. Questions were whis-pered, the answers were flung back carefully on the wisp of a song. At last the owner of the plantation appeared on the veranda. The silence was oppressive and thick with unasked questions and unvoiced fears. Finally the master spoke.

"If any of you-all know where that ole sow Judy is hidin', you can tell her to come on in. Ah don't aim to beat her no mo' but Ah'm sellin' her on down the river. Now get on back to the field!"

The slaves turned and ran back to their work. The ugly mask of fear was torn from their faces. It was as though they had glimpsed daylight for the first time after a million years of darkness. That day a new song was born on the Hopgood plantation. It was a simple song but filled with meaning:

> Hit's a hard road, chillun,
> Hit's a hard road, chillun,
> Hit's a hard road, chillun,
> Hit's a hard road, chillun,
> But dere's joy, joy, comin' bye an' bye.
>
> De Hebrew chillun went through fiah,
> Crossed ovah Jordan an' didn't nevah tiah,
> Caise dey knew Jehovah was in de sky
> An' dere's joy, joy, comin' bye an' bye.
>
> Hit's a long road, chillun,
> Hit's a long road, chillun,
> Hit's a long road, chillun,
> But dere's joy, joy, comin' bye an' bye.

The next morning Judy walked into the backyard of the big house. Two days later she left the plantation for a nearby auction block. She was chained to an ox cart but her head was high.

Dad's grandfather, Major, could have been over the other slaves on the Winston plantation. He could chop more cotton and lift more weight than any other man in the county, but he didn't have sense enough to keep his master informed as to what was going on.

An idea no bigger than the point of a pin fell into his slow mind one day. It grew and grew until there was no room for anything else. "Freedom, freedom, freedom," was the only sound chopped out by his hoe. In the early morning the familiar cock-a-doodle-do of the rooster changed to say, "Up north a man's free." This dangerous new idea, searching through unused passages of Major's mind, stumbled upon an old, old picture. It was buried beneath the dust and confusion of the years. The picture spoke vaguely of big forests and tall trees, of amber sunlight making patterns on the dank floor of the forests, of prowling beasts and brave warriors, of puberty rites and tribal weddings.

Suddenly Major knew with shining clearness that freedom was his right—that it was every man's right. He started out to find it. He had heard the slaves whispering about a "war to set us free." Eluding slave hunters and the Confederate army, he reached the lines of the Yankee soldiers. A small detachment of cavalrymen were being sent up to Cairo, Illinois. They had no horse for the runaway slave but they offered him protection if he could keep up with them.

A week later Major fell exhausted on free soil. He had reached Island Number 10. Those who looked at him smiled warmly as they threw a patchwork quilt over the weary body.

"What did da new one bring?" one slave inquired.

"Chile, he ain't brung nothin' but de rags he wore on his back," an old woman answered.

But Major was wiser than they. He still held his dream— a bright golden vision that glowed and sparkled, warm and alive and comforting. In his heart he held the only thing that had sustained him as he panted and trotted along with the cavalry horses—his desire for freedom.

Dad's mother, Frances, was a tall angular black woman. Her stern features and high cheekbones bespoke a predomi-

nant Indian ancestry. She had the eyes of a mystic. She did
not smile often. She had looked upon horrible things. As
a young wife she had seen a man hang whose only crimes
were being black and being a friend of a murder suspect
who had escaped. She loved beauty and wanted her children
to acquire an education. She was the first Negro woman
in Du Quoin to purchase an organ and outfit her living
room with mohair furniture and Brussels carpets.

Len Berkley, Dad's father, couldn't have read his name
if the letters had been as big as box cars. He worked at Old
Enterprise mines during the day, plowed his ten acres by
moonlight, and could figure faster in his head than Old
Man Smith, the banker, could figure with paper and pen-
cil. He knew dozens of chapters in the Bible from memory
and had hundreds of texts at his finger tips, giving accurately
chapter and verse. He was a minister and was respected by
everyone in the town. One of his staunchest friends was a
little short German shoemaker, Henry Stoutenberg, who
used rather explosive language. His conversation with
Grandfather Berkley was a continual apology.

"You know, Brother Stoutenberg," Grandfather would
admonish, "You shouldn't take the Lord's name in vain."

"I know, goddammit, I mean, excuse me, Len, by God."
Grandfather would listen with attention and toleration, for
as soon as Mr. Stoutenberg became interested in putting
over a point, a stream of curse words would naturally slip
out. Then he would send a thin forceful stream of tobacco
juice toward the dirty cuspidor beside his cobbler's bench
and begin apologizing all over again.

Mother's people had seen life from a different perspec-
tive. Her father, Elijah Holmes, had been set free when his

master died. He was only nine years old at the time; so under the terms of the will, a guardian was appointed for "Lija" as he was called.

When Elijah was thirteen years old, he jumped from a hay shelter and injured his right leg. Although the boy limped about the plantation for a few days, no serious thought was given to the leg until the cook noticed that it was swollen. Finally, when the doctor was called in, he informed them that the leg was infected and would have to be taken off. Elijah stubbornly shook his head.

"He's free," his guardian told the doctor. "I can't tell you to go ahead and take it off. He'll have to decide."

"I'll drop around in a day or so." The doctor smiled at the little brown boy, then beckoned for the guardian to follow him to his carriage. "That leg will have to come off." He did not mince words once he was out of the boy's hearing.

"But I told you the truth. I can't give you the order to do it."

"Does the boy like you?"

"I think he does. I've tried to be good to him."

"Then you should persuade him to let me operate. He won't live if I don't. I'll be driving this way tomorrow." The doctor spoke to his driver, and the carriage pulled out of the big yard.

The guardian walked slowly back to the bench where Lija sat. "Lija, I'd like to ask you a question. Have I always been square with you?"

"Yes suh, always."

"I never lied to you, Lija."

"No suh. Leastways, not as Ah knows of."

"Then you will have to believe me now, Lija."

The guardian sat down on the bench and placed his arm affectionately about the boy's shoulders. "The doctor says he'll have to cut your leg off." The words were said softly but the man could feel the boy shrinking with fear. There were a few seconds of silence; then the boy spoke. His words were so low the man had to bend his head to hear them.

"But, Mister Johnson, Ah won't nevah be able to run no mo'. Ah cain't play wid the odder boys no mo'."

"You'll be able to run again, Lija. Maybe not so fast as before, but a little. You'll play some too. If you don't, Lija, the doctor says you won't—you will—well, you may not live long." It was finally said.

"You mean Ah mought die?"

"Yes, Lija." Suddenly all tension was gone from the little body.

"Well, Ah sho don' wanna do that!" Lija was so positive the guardian smiled in spite of himself.

"Then it will be all right if the doctor comes back tomorrow."

"Yes suh, Mister Johnson. That is effen you stay by me."

The next day Lija was strapped to the wooden bench. The slaves stood grouped together at a distance. While the doctor did his work Aunt Lucindy wiped the tears that gushed from Lija's eyes as the lad gripped the hands of his guardian and friend.

When Lija was able to hobble about the plantation he became apprentice to a shoemaker. He learned to make all kinds of shoes and boots, often adding a bit of hand-tooled decoration to their tops. He was also privileged to take lessons with the young master when the tutor came. In a short time he had learned to read and was assisting the young master who found no pleasure in schoolwork.

When Lija became a young man he courted a shy copper-colored girl on a nearby plantation. This girl, Sarah Ann, could sew beautifully. She was one of the few house servants trusted to iron her young mistress' fluted and ruffled dresses. When Lija asked for Sarah Ann's hand in marriage, he was not only given permission to marry her, but she was given her freedom. Lija made the furniture for their little cabin. Sarah made curtains and hung them at the windows, planted flowers at the door and began keeping house. She was the only colored girl on the big Georgia plantation who was her own mistress.

Because of his freedom and education, most of the slaves looked to Lija to settle their disputes and to give them counsel. Being serious about the trust placed in him, it seemed only natural that Grandfather Holmes should become a minister, too. He served as itinerant preacher throughout the south before he was invited to Du Quoin to run a revival. He and Sarah Ann decided to settle there.

Len and Frances Berkley had acquired a large holding of property to the south of town. From the first Len was intrigued by this peg-legged preacher with the arms and shoulders of a lumberjack. His admiration increased as Elijah stood in the pulpit week after week and read from the Bible or quoted the sayings of John Bunyan, Martin Luther, John Wesley, and even the infidel, Bob Ingersoll. The two men soon became fast friends.

Elijah had been in Du Quoin only three months when Sarah Ann, tired out with much child bearing and supplementing the many times uncertain salary of a minister, died in childbirth. Not until then did Elijah send south to Jackson, Mississippi, to bring his daughter Sophia to Du Quoin. Sophia, who was thirteen years old, had been left with an older sister Della, to attend school and assist with Della's children. Upon her slight shoulders fell the care of the younger children and the parsonage. Because of scarlet fever, her hair had been cropped close like a boy's and she found herself often used as the butt of jokes by the towns-girls who boasted of being "high yellows" with long hair.

Sophia's champion became big Braxton Berkley, an over-grown youngster who had quit school after completing the fourth grade to work in the mines. If Braxton liked anyone or anything, nobody was going to kick him or her or it around. He was very popular with the girls, and when he voiced his disapproval of their ridicule of Sophia, it stopped immediately.

For several years, outspoken Braxton who would fight at the drop of a hat, worshipped Sophia from the sidelines. If she were in a crowd, you could always find him on the outskirts of it. If she were at a church social, he would always appear in time to treat all the girls and eat a dish of ice cream with Sophia.

When Sophia was seventeen, Braxton announced to all the boys that he was going to marry Sophia and to keep hands off. Later he asked Sophia.

The Berkleys were a little perturbed, for the Holmes family had nothing but a good reputation. True, Elder Holmes was still pastor of Mt. Zion Baptist Church, but even now there were mutterings and a group of the members were strongly in favor of starting another church. Ida and Lucy Berkley, who dressed nicer than most of the colored girls in town, admitted that Sophia's clothes were shoddy, but she was a "nice" girl and came from a good family.

Even though the Holmes family could not match the Berkleys in mohair furniture and Brussels carpets, you couldn't look down your nose at a girl whose oldest brother played a pipe organ in a big white church, who had an exclusive portrait studio in St. Louis, where only the fashionable and rich sat for their pictures, and whose oldest sister tutored the children of rich planters in Jackson, Mississippi. What Sophia Holmes lacked in worldy goods, she made up for in education and cultural background.

Len Berkley built a four-room house on an acre of ground and gave it to them as a wedding present.

"It ain't much, but it's something for a starter," he said, as he handed them the keys to the spanking brand-new house.

In that brand-new house Braxton and Sophia Berkley began to build their own family, and in that building no one contributed a more helping hand than Dr. Gillis whose ministry of healing encompassed three generations of Berkleys.

Dr. Gillis had stood by the bed of Grandmother Frances, in her last moments, still grieving for her youngest son Job who had died among strangers. Trying to comfort the family, his voice was harsh with emotion. "Frances is a strong woman, and I could pull her through in spite of her sixty-three years, if she had the will to live. There isn't a pill or prescription in the world that can cure a broken heart."

"I'd a felt better if he had a died at home," Grandmother Frances muttered, as they looked on, "but mah pore baby died among strangers—died among strangers—nobody he knowed there to hold his han'. Mah po' baby—Mah po' baby." Then suddenly the muttering ceased and Grandmother Frances had crossed over Jordan to join her baby.

Sensing Grandpa Len's loneliness, Dr. Gillis fell into the habit of dropping by to chat for a few minutes whenever his calls brought him into the Bottoms. Then one day he didn't stay long. He listened to Grandpa Len minimize an ailment that would restrict him to the house "Jes for a few days, Doc." He left a few pills on the marble-top table by the bed, then went into the kitchen where Aunt Ida and Uncle Robert sat talking. His eyes were watery, and he kept blowing his nose. When he could trust his voice, he said, "Let him have anything he wants to eat, Ida. My old friend won't be with us much longer."

Years later, a group of race zealots waited on Mother and Dad, soliciting support for our first Negro doctor, Zephaniah Green, who came to Du Quoin fresh from a southern medical school.

"Take the white man's hand out of yore pocket!" the long-winded spokesman ended.

Dad and Mother looked at each other. "Dr. Gillis is a fair man," Dad defended. "It's given out he's the best doctor in southern Illinois. If his hand is in your pocket, he's jus' takin' what belongs to him."

"Braxton is right," Mother backed Dad up. "We never stop to think whether Dr. Gillis is white, black, or purple. He's our friend, and that's all there is to it." And that was the word with the bark on it. Thus, Dr. Gillis, like the once spanking new house, was of our past as well as of our present.

With the exception of a few short months when we moved in with Aunt Ida because she was ill, Grandpa Berkley's wedding present to Dad and Mother was our home. This little house was the hub of all the activities in the Bottoms. Its windows looked out on many sights. Its walls were the confessional for many troubled people. It knew life and death, love and hate. It was the refuge of tramps and the conference room of a governor.

6. Sunday morning

Willie Turner was Dad's cousin. He was short, black, and bow-legged, with a perpetual smile and an infectious sense of humor. He should have been on the stage. To us he was much funnier than Bert Williams, who came to St. Louis every year with the Ziegfeld Follies. Some of the older people accused him of being stingy with his money. Maybe he was, but he was a spendthrift with the world's highest commodity—wholesome humor.

As soon as we heard his voice, we scampered screaming from everywhere and crowded about him.

"Get away from Willie," Mother admonished. "You'll get him dirty. Make them get down, Willie."

But Willie never seemed to mind. Taking us by the hand he would form a circle and dance us around the room while he chanted his favorite poem from the old McGuffey Reader:

> Oh come with me and we will go
> To try the winter's cold, sir,
> 'Tis freezing now and soon will snow,
> But we are tough and bold, sir.

"Lord, Willie, these children take you for a regular plaything. You'd better come on and let me tie your tie before I start making up my biscuits and get my hands all covered with flour."

Sunday morning

Willie had never learned how to tie his tie. He came over every Sunday morning for Mama to do it for him. Since then, I have suspected that he only used the tie as a ruse to come over and play with us. After Mother had adjusted the four-in-hand at the proper angle, she went back to her cooking. Again Willie turned his attention to his enslaved audience. He bowed, squatted, swayed, pranced, and moved his hands with slow rhythmic grace as he recited poem after poem from memory. We had heard them all many, many times—*The Spider and the Fly, Over the River, The Little Match Girl,* and *We Are Seven.* We sat quietly, following his flow of artistry with a tightening of our throats and tears in our eyes as he recreated the poverty of the little girl trudging from door to door selling matches; the loneliness of the child who would not recognize the separation of death and insisted that there were still seven in her family though some were buried in the churchyard and some were lost at sea.

Breaking the tragic spell he would then spring out the front door singing with accompanying gestures:

> We'll chase the antelope over the plain,
> And the tiger's cub we'll bind with a chain——

Again we were laughing. Willie wobbled on across the road to his home where he lived with Cousin Frankie and her quiet sister, Nettie, who kept a cookie jar that was never empty.

Sunday morning also brought Uncle George across the road with a tempting just-right-brown chicken drumstick in his hand. Uncle George was the town constable. He was what you might call a weather-beaten mulatto. His hair was not close cropped, neither did it hang on his neck in Daniel

Boone fashion. His trim mustache was slightly curled at each end, and long before I had ever seen a Kentucky colonel, long, lean, slightly stooped, Uncle George typified that gentry to me.

He was married to Dad's oldest sister, Belle, and they lived in a gray frame house directly across the street from us.

Uncle George could not read and could only write his name, but nobody knew this but the older folk of the family. We never questioned why Mother always read over his warrants for arrest or papers of eviction. Sometimes she would make out as many as ten rent receipts. Uncle George would sign them, collect the money, give each renter his proper receipt, and never make a mistake.

Like most people who are short on book learning, Uncle George had a remarkable memory. He would listen very attentively while Mother read the warrant over to him. Then he would sally forth, gun in holster, and warrant or court summons in hand, and read it off to the party for whom it was intended without omitting one single "to wit" or "whereas."

Uncle George didn't have any teeth. His breakfast consisted largely of mush, but Aunt Belle fried a chicken every Sunday morning.

"Hello, Sophia. Hello, there," he greeted Helen and me. "Where's Braxton?"

"He went up to Ida's," Mother answered. "Come in and sit down."

"Where's Spud and Cecil? Oh, there you are." He moved the drumstick closer to his mouth. "Now don't ask me for this chicken. If you ask me for it, I won't give you one bite."

64

Spud and Cecil looked at each other, then back to Uncle George.

"Let me see how quiet you can be this morning. Sit over there, both of you. Now the one who don't move till I say so, I'll give him a nickel."

"Do we have to keep still all over?" Cecil, knowing Uncle George, wanted all the rules, which were sure to be changed or modified if the first conditions were met.

"I don't want you to move even an eyebrow," Uncle George cautioned.

They took their seats, Uncle George sitting across the room from the two boys. The endurance contest was on. Spud and Cecil stared straight ahead while Uncle George threatened to bite into the chicken.

"I saw you swallow, Cecil. I saw you."

"I didn't move nothing. The swallow just slid down. I didn't do it."

"Yes, he did, Uncle George," Spud accused, pointing a finger at Cecil.

"What are you jumping up about. I told you not to move—not to move an eyebrow. Neither one of you is going to get nothing." He whistled for Prince who came to the door, lifting his beautiful head and wagging his tail. "Want a nice piece of chicken, Prince?"

"Give it to me, Uncle George," Spud begged.

"Didn't your mama and papa teach you not to be begging people for food? Folks that didn't know you would think that Sophia didn't cook enough."

Both Spud and Cecil were feeling very sorry for themselves by now. Uncle George always knew when their spirits were lowest. At this point, he would take two nickels from his pocket, and pushing one into each chubby hand, he

65

would hold fast to them and take them back across the road to his house. Soon they would be coming around the path, each grinning broadly and nibbling on a piece of fried chicken.

"What are you doing over to our house eating up my breakfast," Ernest, Uncle George's son, yelled good naturedly at them. They smiled and kept on eating. By this time Mother had two iron skillets full of chicken on the kitchen stove. The hot grease bubbled and the floured meat was turning a golden brown. Dad had come back from Aunt Ida's, and Mother was taking a last peek at the biscuits.

"Mama, here comes Francis X. Bushman," Helen announced. We called Ernest by the name of the then current matinee idol. He was a tall, copper-colored young man. He walked proudly and always looked as if he were advertising Werner's Men's Store. His mustache was heavy, but he wore it neatly trimmed. His pointed nose was made for the pair of nose glasses he wore.

"Sophia, how does this tie go with my suit?" he asked Mother.

"It's a perfect match," Mother told him.

"Then I guess I'll be going on. Gotta catch a train. Going to see Maude today."

"Going to St. Louis?" Dad asked. Maude, Ernest's only sister, was a seamstress in the city.

"Just for the day. Why don't you come on and go, Uncle Brax?"

"Didn't know you were going." Dad was always ready to travel. "Anyway I promised the kids I'd take them to Sunday school."

"Ernest knows he looks all right," Mother said when

66

Ernest was across the street. "He always looks nice. I think he comes over so we can tell him so."

"He hears that enough from the girls in St. Louis." Dad stated the obvious fact with just a tinge of regret in his voice.

"Here comes a tramp around the house," Spud whispered.

"Hush," Mother cautioned. "You must never let people hear you call them names. I do declare, I think they have this house marked."

"Most likely they smelled the chicken from the railroad track," Dad said with a smile.

There was a hesitant knock at the door. Dad was a sucker for a touch.

"Kind sir, I am hungry. I haven't had a bite to eat in three days."

"They all say that," Cecil whispered to Spud. Both of them giggled.

"I hate to ask for anything," the tramp continued, "but you look like a kind man. Most Negroes are kind. Kinder than the white folks. Just yesterday I stopped in Elksville. Went to the back door of one of my own people and they ran me out of the yard."

Mother had just put the chicken on the platter. We were ready to sit down to breakfast.

"Here's the wash pan. Maybe you'd like to wash up a bit." Dad gave the tramp the wash basin with water, soap, and a towel.

"You're God's own gentleman. I ain't a common tramp," the man's voice was muffled as he rubbed his hands over his face. "I am a worker. All I want is a job."

"Ever do any mining?" Dad asked casually.

"Mining? Why I was the best entry driver in Franklin County." The tramp had washed his face and was now seated on the back porch in a chair Dad had offered him. Dad came back into the house and took the platter of chicken and the plate of biscuits from the stove. Mother looked her disapproval, but he took them on out on the porch and held them in front of the tramp.

"Help yourself."

The tramp was so profuse with his thanks we momentarily expected him to get down on his knees and salaam three times to Dad.

"If you're interested in a job, I'm sure you can get on at the mines. We need good entry drivers. Of course, you'll have to join the union. Everybody does; black, white, grizzly, or gray. You see, we protect each other by having the union. Every man has the same voice. There are no big I's and little you's."

"It's kind of you, brother, but I am on my way home. I had a letter last week from my poor old mother. She ain't expected to live. Thanks for the food and for treating me human." The tramp shuffled on around the corner of the house.

"I hope you find your mother better," Dad called to him.

"You know he's lying. I'll bet his mother's been dead for years," Mother snatched the platter of chicken from Dad's hands and put it back in the oven to warm.

"I know, but it didn't hurt none to make him think we believe in him. A man ain't never poor if he thinks somebody got faith in him. Come on children, let's pray."

Sunday morning prayer was a ritual at our house. We all bowed upon our knees, while Dad at the head of the table approached the throne of grace.

68

"This morning, our Heavenly Father, it is once more that Your humble servant has come before You, thanking You for the many blessings You have bestowed upon us and begging You to have mercy upon us.

"As we bow before You this morning, we thank You that we are clothed, and in our right mind, and have a reasonable portion of our health and strength. We thank Thee that Thou hast kept us from all hurt, harm, and danger of sin.

"We ask You to be with us, Lord, in every undertaking of life. Bring peace out of confusion, light out of darkness, strength out of weakness. Be our shield, and hiding place, and our eternal home.

"Thou knowest all about us. Thou knowest our hearts and our heart's desire. Thou knowest when we would do good; evil is always present. Satan and his host have declared the good we seek we shall not obtain, but we do thank Thee that Thou art a God whose proclamation is always to have mercy; so we beg Thee to have mercy upon us this morning.

"We know that You can open doors, and no man can shut them; You can work wonders and no man can hinder. Be with us, Lord, picking and choosing our various changes, fronting and fighting our many battles in life. Beat back the clouds of darkness that overshadow our path and bid our golden moments to roll on a while longer.

"Now bless us, Altogether Lovely. Bless our friends and relatives wherever they may be. Bless the sick and the afflicted, the distressed and oppressed in body and mind. Bless the widows and the orphans, the prison and the prison-bound.

"Give us more grace, and more faith, and a better understanding how to suit and to serve Thee. And when it comes ours to swap time for eternity, give us a home in Thy kingdom where we can praise Thy name forever. These favors we ask in the name of Him who taught us to pray—Our Father, who art in heaven . . ."

The Lord's Prayer was beautiful and touching as it fell from Dad's lips.

We repeated slowly after him, though all of us knew the prayer from memory. The kitchen was warm and quiet. We were cemented together by the strong bonds of faith and love.

"For Thine is the kingdom, and the power, and the glory forever. Amen."

7. *we become a race of champions*

Two things of world-wide importance happened in 1910. Halley's comet swept across the heavens dragging its nebulous tail, and Jack Johnson fought Jim Jeffries in Reno, Nevada. The first brought with it fear born of unscientific speculation. The effects of the comet were temporary and fleeting. For weeks the papers had talked about it. Artists had drawn spectacular pictures of the fiery body crashing to earth. The churches did a wholesale business with backsliders and sinners standing in line to kneel at the altars. Ordinary Christians became saints as zealous gentlemen of the cloth warned everybody to "flee from wrath to come."

One night in April it appeared suddenly in the sky, outranking in magnitude every other star. It was awe-inspiring as it marched majestically across the heavens. For weeks everybody sat out on their front porches, or hung over their fences, and watched the comet until their necks were stiff or their backs were sore. Then they politely nodded good night to each other, said their prayers, and went to bed wondering if they would live the night through. But you can get used to anything.

After a few weeks, people reverted to normal. Neighborhood squabbles, fights, and Saturday night drinking sprees came back into vogue. Alma Flagg and Ole Lady Brickels "played the dozens" across the back fence. The people along the tracks started stealing coal again from the loaded cars

71

in the north end. The Kingdom of God had receded, and Du Quoin became its dear, uninhibited self once again.

The Jeffries-Johnson fight had been cooked up by that wizard of boxing promotion, Tex Rickard. Jim Jeffries was from Carrol, Ohio. He has often been referred to as the "strongest man in the ring." He possessed tremendous stamina and by 1904 he had fought himself out of opponents. Internationally, Tommy Burns of Australia became the acknowledged champion, but when Jack Johnson defeated Burns, Rickard and a few other smart boys labeled Jeffries "the white hope" and started to work on the old fighter's ego. Jeffries agreed to meet the young Negro fighter in an outdoor arena at Reno on July fourth.

Every Fourth of July the Holmes clan spent the day with Aunt Judith and Uncle Charlie Thompson. Aunt Tolitha and Uncle Tobe brought their children; Grandpa Holmes and Miz Cordelia brought their two youngsters, Gilbert and Emery. We accompanied Mother, for Dad was taking care of the lunch counter in Mr. John Simmon's pool hall. He very seldom went to the family reunions anyway, for he was an ardent baseball fan, and when he wasn't playing himself, he and Cousin Babe, Willie Turner, and Ernest Smith caught the St. Louis-Cairo short line and went to St. Louis to see the Cardinals or the Giants. No matter what the outcome, the thing they discussed most was not the merits of the individual players comprising the teams. They discussed the insanity of American race prejudice that kept Rube Foster out of big league competition.

Sometimes Uncle John and Aunt Stella would bring their family. There were always a few close neighbors who came over, and Belle Woodson, Uncle Charlie's sister who looked like a dark Egyptian princess. The Holmes family did not face extinction, for sterility, along with murder, was looked upon as a cardinal sin. Children were everywhere. They banged on the oblong-shaped grand piano in the parlor, overflowed the house, pushed each other off the benches under the grape arbor, pulled the half-green plums that hung over the fence from Effie Boner's yard, and trampled the few clusters of Shasta daisies that made a heroic but losing battle to beautify the fence along Park Street.

Ordinarily, Grandpa Holmes was the acknowledged head of any family gathering. The children all loved him, the older folks respected him. He was a marvelous storyteller and historian, an excellent judge of human nature. On a picnic he could stand in one place and catch enough fish for the entire crowd. No matter how we threw our lines around or over his, sometimes tangling them all up, he patiently untangled the lines, warned us about the viciousness of hooks, threw his line back into the creek and quickly pulled out another fish.

"Don't make so much noise, children." He would say sometimes as an afterthought, "the fish don't like noise."

Today Grandpa Holmes was content to sit back and concede the place of honor to Grandma Thompson. Uncle Charlie's mother was only four feet, ten inches tall. She was ninety-seven years old and walked with short mincing steps. You didn't have to yell to make her hear, and she could read a newspaper without the aid of glasses. Age had not made her bitter and had only mellowed her wit. This, I am sure, was more appreciated by the older people than by the children. We were chiefly awed by her physical aspect.

Grandma Thompson's snow white hair was slowly but surely turning black again. That very morning she had stood before the washstand in her room, and there in a mouth that had been toothless for years, the point of a new tooth was pushing itself through her gums!

Ordinarily, the day was spent in playing games and eating. Toward evening we would all squeeze into the parlor, and there Uncle John would direct us in songs ranging from ballads to the classics. Maybe a ball game or a round of croquet would be played, but usually we took the day leisurely with the accent on eating. Each family brought a large box or hamper filled with fried chicken, barbecued ribs, potato salad, fresh tomatoes, cakes, and pies of all descriptions. There was always a large iron pot of boiling water filled with Golden Bantam corn. Conversation was spirited among the older folks and sometimes ended in a heated argument.

Today, however, the grownups all seemed preoccupied. If a question was asked, it had to be repeated two or three times. That is, all but one question.

"What time is it out there, now?" always received a quick reply, as the time teller quickly computed the difference between central and western time.

Uncle Charlie always had to be cautioned about his stomach trouble after he had eaten his third or fourth drumstick and a couple of slices of lemon pie. But today Uncle Charlie wasn't eating. Finally, the tension made itself felt among the children.

"Why's everybody looking like a funeral is going on?" one of the kids wanted to know.

"Don't show your ignorance," Charlie cautioned. "Don't you know Jack Johnson is fighting Jim Jeffries today?"

"That ain't nothing," Anderson, who was much younger,

74

piped up. "Mr. Mendenhall fights his wife every Saturday night. You ought to hear her holler."

"You're full of prunes." Charles brushed him off.

"I ain't. We didn't have any prunes for breakfast."

"Every time you open your mouth you don't display your teeth—you display your ignorance."

"That's all right," Anderson defended, "you ought to be smart. Your head's long enough."

"Just you leave my head alone," Charles snapped. "You wouldn't take no beauty prize at the county fair."

"At that, I ain't as ugly as you. Boy, you know, when you die you ain't gonna get sick. You jus' gonna ugly away."

"I don't care Mr. Good-looking. Beauty's only skin deep, ugly's to the bone; beauty soon will fade away, but ugly holds its own," Charles recited. He gave Anderson a playful backhand lick, and they started chasing each other through the yard.

"It'll be the first time in the history of the world," Uncle Tobe said with emphasis. Uncle Tobe was a soft-spoken, mild-mannered little fellow.

"That's taking in a lot of territory, Tobe," Uncle John reminded him. "We've had lots of great fighters. In the olden times, a fellow named Hannibal was quite a scrapper."

"I heard of him," Uncle Tobe shot back. "He used elephants and nearly scared the Romans to death. I ain't talking about them times. I'm talking about in these modern days. This is the first time to my knowing that a colored man had the chance to stand in a ring with a white man and fight for the heavyweight championship of the world."

That was quite a long speech for Uncle Tobe. I am sure Jack Johnson had no idea of the magic he was sprinkling over the entire Negro population. In far away Nevada a tall black boxer with the build of Apollo had touched meek Uncle Tobe's tongue with flaming oratory.

Little Arthur, as Jack was sometimes called, had probably forgotten that he had ever heard of Du Quoin. Dad had met him in St. Louis when Jack first began his barnstorming tour that finally landed him in the squared circle opposite the Herculean figure of Jim Jeffries. They called them battle royals in the old days. A young, up-and-coming fighter was put in the ring with a number of opponents. This night, Dad had puffed on a stogie and watched this young black boy from Galveston, Texas, send six opponents sprawling on the canvas. Those who weren't knocked out, crawled through the ropes away from the murderous fists of the fighter. Nobody had laid a glove on him as he pranced and squatted about the ring.

"Fella"—Dad slapped Jack on the shoulder as they sat in Dick Kemp's club after the fights—"that was a great scrap. You really had to do some turning to keep from getting hit."

"Brack," the young fighter grinned, "I ain't never been hurt in my life. Geemanelly, I don't believe there's a man living that can whup me. I ain't just saying it, either. If I ever get a chance at Jeffries, you put every penny you can get on me. I'll bring home the bacon."

Today it was actually coming to pass. Dad didn't have much money on the fight. You couldn't find much Jeffries money. What few dollars the white men were willing to wager to uphold their belief in white supremacy was quickly snapped up by the Negroes and Italians. But there was more at stake than just a few dollars. The fate of an entire race hung in the balance. Today, one lone black man had the power to make us a race of champions.

"Helen," Mother called, "you and Ruby run down to the pool hall and see if Braxton has sold out. If he has, tell him to come on over and get his dinner."

Dad ran his lunch counter like a bargain sale. He cooked once a day. When that was all served the lunch counter automatically closed.

"You don't need to go in. Just ask some of the men to tell your father to come outside."

Soon we were skipping along Maple Street. At Bolden's store we turned east on Main Street. Clusters of people stood about the streets. The same air of expectancy we had noticed at Aunt Judith's, hovered over the street. When we reached the pool hall all the tables were idle. Dad and all the men stood on the sidewalk near the door.

"A white man is the biggest coward on the face of the earth," someone said as we neared the group of men.

"In the South it takes two or three hundred of 'em to lynch one unarmed nigger."

"Things gonna be different after while. In the Bible it says, 'Ethiopia gonna stretch forth her wings.' When she do, look out, white man."

Dad stepped out from the group.

"Want something?" he inquired.

"Mama wanted to know if you had sold out. She said dinner was ready over to Aunt Judith's," Helen answered.

"I ain't sold nothing. Nobody's got any appetite. Everybody's waiting to see how the fight comes out."

"Think Mr. Jack Johnson will win?" I asked.

"Well, I don't know," Dad said thoughtfully. "Jeffries is as strong as a bull and he packs a mean wallop, but," here Dad paused for a few seconds, "Jack is a clever boxer. He's shifty and hard to hit. If Jeffries fools around and lets him

77

land an uppercut—I believe my boy will win. Run along now; tell Sophia I'll come as soon as I sell out."

Dad's assurance was all we needed. We ran back to Aunt Judith's with the electrifying news that Jack Johnson had won.

"How do you know?" Grandpa Holmes questioned.

"It ain't time yet," Sam Stigall looked at his watch.

"Well, Papa said he believes he'll win," I said stoutly.

"What Braxton believes and what Jack Johnson will do is altogether different," Miss Belle remarked.

"Braxton usually knows what he's talking about," Mother defended.

"I believe he'll win if it's a fair fight," Uncle Tobe was hopeful.

"What do you mean, a fair fight?" Aunt Tolitha wanted to know.

"Well, someone can buy the referee off, or maybe they'll dope the water they give Jack Johnson," Uncle Tobe explained. "But I'm like Braxton, I believe if they let 'em stand up there toe to toe and fight it out, I believe Johnson will win. A black man is as good as a white man any day."

"The white man knows you're as good as, if not better than he is. He just don't want you to find it out," Grandma Thompson silenced further argument.

A few minutes later the little town became alive. A group of men who had hung about the offices of the Du Quoin *Call* rushed out of the building and down the street spreading the news.

Jack Johnson, a Negro, was heavyweight champion of the world!

The Negroes were jubilant. Everybody wanted to buy someone else a dinner, a glass of beer, or a shot of whiskey.

Jerome Banks who had lost his leg in a mine accident, came down the street waving one of his crutches and his short stump in the air. The older people laughed and cried, and the children danced around and knocked each other about in good fun. Grandma Thompson stood under the grape arbor and raised her quivering voice in song. We all joined in:

"Hallelujah, hallelujah, the storm is passing over, halle-lujah!"

Little Arthur had delivered. We were now a race of champions!

8. *when the black spider crawled*

Death is a black spider that creeps into every house no matter how strongly built. At first we heard only a vague rumor as the east coast of the country staggered, gasped, and died like flies from a strange sickness called Spanish Influenza. Suspicion pushed along the report that the Germans, though defeated on the battle fields of France and forced into a reluctant armistice, had retaliated by loosing a bomb filled with deadly disease germs.

As the spider moved on long legs down city streets and country lanes, mothers interrupted snow fights and the making of rotund snow men to snatch their children into the safety of a warm house. Youthful skaters, spelling their names and making figure eights on the frozen pond by Blakesley's Foundry, heeded the shrill calls of frightened parents. With keen-edged skates thrown over their shoulders or dangling at their sides, they went homeward sullenly, furious at the older generation that was worn out and frightened with life.

The billboards went unchanged in front of the Lyric Theatre. The bright lights in the marquee were winked out by order of Charlie Layman, chief of police. Schools were closed and the people who ventured on the streets were grotesquely masked with protective coverings of medicated gauze tied over their noses.

We were an island unto ourselves, but even though every

family barricaded itself behind its weather-beaten doors, old death kept creeping in. The slate-colored hearse of Charlie Weinberg was a familiar sight, and each family had to meet its Gethsemane alone. There were no wakes where friends sat throughout the night, drinking strong coffee and raking through the ashes of a dimly remembered past to retell a story of the kindness, humor, or bravery of the departed. There were no church services with doleful songs and long eulogies.

We would have been more easily reconciled to the passing of Freeman Sampson if he had been one of the many victims of the flu. His death in a mine accident, however, was a backhanded lick that shocked the town. No matter how long you live in a mining town, no matter how many times you hear of slides of slate or cave-ins, or the viciousness of the blind mules that pull the dwarf cars of coal to the main entries, you are never ready for the sudden death that strikes a man down in the bowels of the earth. The last time I saw Freeman Sampson alive he was clutching the little Sunday school bell in his hands and walking aimlessly through the crowd that watched the burning church. The next time I saw him he was lying straight and stiff in a gray velours casket, his dark features overcast by the shadow of death. Freeman had been crushed by a hanging ledge of coal that he was going to prop up as soon as he finished loading his fifth car. But the coal wouldn't wait. As Freeman was placing the last chunk on top of the car, the hanging ledge tore itself impatiently from the ceiling with a splitting, rumbling noise.

Miners from the adjoining rooms rushed in, heaving and pulling at the jagged pieces of coal until their hands oozed blood. Their black dusty clothing, wet with perspiration and the "bleeding" of the coal, clung damp and soggy to their straining bodies. The flicker of the carbide lamps, fastened to their caps, filled the room with dancing shadows. They knew as they lifted the huge pieces of coal that there could be no life in the body pinned beneath it. They worked furiously, cursing the coal for its wanton destruction and cursing themselves for being fools enough to work at such a dangerous job. Yet each knew that tomorrow would find him back in the narrow entry going gaily to his little underground room that was as familiar to him as his own house.

We stood about in the Sampson yard, not close together as people huddle in the face of a great sorrow. We stood a few feet apart, as the law required.

Lizzie Sampson sat quiet and stunned. Her full lips quivered as she held her four-year-old son, Harold, and gently patted his slight shoulder. Harold was a queer child. Cousin Frankie said he must have been born with a veil over his face which blessed him with second sight. The things he lisped had an uncomfortable way of coming true. Blessed or cursed, we never knew. For is it better to sing in the shadow of an unknown terror or to go timidly forth and wait for the nameless evil to blot out your sun?

On the morning of the accident, long before Freeman had been crushed and the dirty miners had tramped into the house laying all that was mortal on Lizzie's log cabin patchwork quilt, Harold had followed her about asking questions for which she had no answer. Questions which filled her with a sense of impending disaster. There had been another morning and other questions before the body of an older brother had been pulled from under a raft on the pond at Will Hayes' ice plant. A weakness had come over Lizzie, and she had sunk wearily into a chair as the insistent voice had kept up the questioning. "Mama, what all these people doin' in our yard? Mama, whatsa madda wid papa?"

With the composure of innocence, Harold looked about at the people who dotted the yard, then back to his mother. His skinny fingers wiped a tear that ran unchecked down his mother's dark cheek as he admonished, "Don't cry, Mama. We won't let nothin' dit you."

Charlie, Laura, Dolly Belle, and Ruth, the four other children, taking their cue from their mother, stood close to each other, whimpering dolefully. There was not a dry eye in the yard. My grief was heavy and confused. Although I knew the crumpled body of Freeman Sampson lay in the casket, it seemed at times that it was my own dad. Then I would try to imagine our family at dinner without Dad's deep voice asking God's blessing on the food. My ears would listen hungrily for the spontaneous prayer chanting as he did the heavier chores in the darkness of early morning before he went to the mines. But the straining was no good. I could not hear Dad's voice above the awful wail of desolation now being intoned by Grandpa Holmes, "Man that is born of woman is of few days and is full of trouble."

I was not conscious of walking through the Sampson gate. When I came to myself I was running blindly across the railroad tracks, the salty taste of tears in my mouth, the shrill whistle of a long freight bearing down from the south was in my ears. Home was now in sight and I burst into the front room looking wildly about for Dad and Mother. The tears had dried, but my breath was still coming in short gasps.

Mother's voice came from her room. "Is that you, Ruby?"

"Yessum," I answered quickly. Looking into her room I

saw her lying in bed. The collar of her gingham dress was visible above the quilts. I realized that she was fully clothed. that her strength had only been sufficient for her to drag herself to where she now lay. I rushed to the bed as a wave of protective tenderness came over me, for a minute stilling the panic of finding her ill.

Mother was too weak to talk, and yet there were things that had to be said. In the washed-out brown of her face only the eyes, tormented and concerned, seemed alive. The hand that lay on top of the cover was limp and purposeless. I leaned nearer to catch the short sentences that came in rasping whispers. "You and Helen will have to manage. No, we can't ask anybody to help us. Take good care of the baby."

I raced to the gashouse again. The figure shoveling coal was not the friendly black Simon we knew so well. A strange white man stood wiping his forehead, his chalky, brown-splotched face streaked with coal dust.

"Sure you can call the doctor, kid." He nodded to the phone. "Your folks got the bug too. Simon's laid up." The voice was warm and reassuring but it did nothing to allay the panic in my heart. Mrs. Gillis' voice came over the wire. It was tired and unconcerned as though sickness no longer mattered—as though nothing no longer mattered. No, the doctor was not in. No, she didn't know when he would be in. No, she didn't know where to find him. I placed the receiver back on the hook and walked slowly out of the gashouse. I must have thanked the man, though I do not remember. The friendly voice followed me out into the waning sunlight, "Sure kid, anytime—anytime." I tried to take consolation in the fact that Mrs. Gillis would send the doctor as soon as he came in. But when would that be? Would it be too late?

Supper consisted of warmed-over food and fruit from the pantry shelves. Because the mines had been working short-handed, Dad had been asked to stay on that night and work as a shot firer. Our cousin, Ernest Smith, had yelled this bit of information across the street before he had turned into his yard. Spud and Cecil did the chores without grumbling. The house was strangely quiet. There seemed to be a chill in the room not to be dispelled by the blazing fire in the base-burner. There were no friendly arguments or fist fights. No feet were stuck deliberately far out to trip someone in passing. From time to time one of us would peek into Mother's room. Frances Ann wakened and whimpered like a cold puppy.

It was nearly ten o'clock when Aunt Dea bustled into the room with a "Name o' God, Sophia, why didn't you send one of the children up for me?" Mama murmured something about not wanting to be any trouble or not wanting anybody to catch what she had.

"Della Crayton jes tole me you wasn't 'sposed to go to anybody's house that was sick. Said the police said not to. I tole her Charlie Layman could run his mouth but he sho couldn't run my business. You kids get to bed. I'll set up with Sophia." She waved the smaller children to bed as though she were shooing chickens from a patch of tender mustard greens. Nightshirts and sleepers were found, and there was real fervour in the "God bless Mama" that heretofore had been a matter-of-fact utterance.

It was after midnight when Dr. Gillis pushed open the front door. There was a stoop in his shoulders and a tired-

85

ness in his voice as he threw his hat and topcoat on a chair. Aunt Dea came from the kitchen with a steaming cloth in her hand. She held it out as though awaiting the doctor's approval. "Mustard plaster," she commented.

"Won't do any harm," Dr. Gillis conceded, though he didn't sound hopeful.

Our old Plymouth Rock rooster had stretched his speckled neck and crowed for day before we heard Dad's slow step on the porch. He had been away for twenty hours. His bronzed features were covered with layers of coal dust. The unlit carbide lamp still fastened to his cap was slightly askew. He was pulling off his heavy short coat when he entered the door. His blue chambray shirt was stiff and circled with perspiration stains. There was a great weariness in his face and the sagging muscles of his body. The day had been a race against time to fill the many always empty cars that rattled up and down the entries. The night was a race with the rows of fuses set to blast the next day's coal from the rocky walls. The shot firer stuck the lighted wick to the fuse, then raced into the entry for safety. This was the most dangerous job in the mines.

His lips were slow to speak but there was a questioning in his eyes when he saw Helen and me fully dressed. As Dr. Gillis came through the door shaking a thermometer, the questioning look changed to apprehension and for the first time in my life I saw fear in Dad's eyes. It was not a personal fear or the fright of a known evil. It was a fear cradled in the lap of the unknown and the inevitable.

Dad said one word, "Sophia?" Aunt Dea had heard him come in and her angular form rushed through the door directly behind Dr. Gillis. She was at Dad's side, taking the heavy coat from his fingers and placing a hand firmly on

86

his arm. "We're doing all we can, Buddy. We're doing all we can."

Dad walked into Mother's room muttering almost inaudibly, "I know—I know." Mother had been asleep, but as Dad bent to touch the hand that lay inert upon the cover, her eyes opened, and for the first time there was a feeble flicker of hope in their amber depths. With a sigh she turned her head wearily on the pillow and went back to sleep.

The hours seemed endless. The lights burned all night in our house. Aunt Dea and Dr. Gillis kept their vigil until the sun, though dimmed by a murky haze, was a faint aluminum disk high in the heavens.

Dad had slipped to his knees, unmindful of his sooty clothes rubbing against the clean quilts. We could not make out the words that he chanted in a low moaning voice. But it didn't matter. After all, he wasn't talking to us. Helen catnapped by the base-burner, her round dark brown face bobbing about.

The blackness of night had crept away before the grayness of early morning. A misty film lay over the town. I went to the window and looked out. This was the dawning of a new day that held no hope. For the black spider still crouched outside, waiting for one of us to fall asleep so that he could crawl through the keyhole.

9. we witness a hanging

We were trailed through childhood by a group of nonde-script animals we called pets. They were Prophet, our horse; Cherry, a Holstein cow; Blizzard and Prince, Dad's prize bird dogs. We didn't think of them as animals. They must have reasoned the same, else how could we account for the night when a blizzard blew the barn door open. We heard intermittent stamping on the back porch and when Dad opened the door, Cherry walked into the kitchen.

There were smaller pets. Cecil kept a white rat in a shoe box under his bed. Bob and Cliff rode herd on a little gopher turtle Aunt Ida brought them from Florida. Spud walked about the yard with a crippled robin perched on his shoulder, and one summer he carried a little garter snake in his coat pocket.

We named numerous chickens and ducks and made such a fuss over them that Mother couldn't kill them for the table. "Be just like eating a member of the family," she'd say, as she pushed them aside and reached for another.

But of all the pets, none ever brought us so much joy and sorrow as did Cora, a fluffy little golden-feathered chicken, and Greyco, whose common alley cat ancestry had had a light brush with Maltese nobility.

One day Cora was running and playing at our heels. The next day her lifeless body was clutched tightly in Greyco's teeth.

Helen was shedding big drops of tears. Cecil dug into his eyes with his chubby fist. Spud blew his nose on the ground, then rubbed his right coat sleeve across it. I stood biting my lips and looking first at the mangled body of Cora, then back to Greyco, who made no attempt to run away from the scene of his crime, or to offer an excuse for this terrible deed.

"Why did you do it, Greyco, why did you do it?" Cecil cried.

"Cora never done nothing to nobody," Helen sobbed. "Mama said he was no good when he came here." She pointed an accusing finger at Greyco, who looked off in the direction of the salt mines that stood at the northwest edge of town.

"You may be too proud to speak now, but I bet when we get through with you, you won't hurt nobody else." Spud picked up a stick.

"No, Spud, that ain't the way we do. We'll have to have his trial. That's the only way—well, I mean, the only right way." Cecil finished lamely.

Spud knocked on a nearby piece of wood.

"Court is now in session, Judge Spud Berkley 'residing. Cecil, you be the defense attorney. Reuben, you be the state's attorney. Helen, you're the witness." Spud always gave the orders.

"I don't wanna talk for Greyco," Cecil whined. "Ole mean thing."

"Me neither," I agreed.

"Somebody has to be on his side," Spud said firmly.

"Oh, all right," I consented, "but let's hurry and get it over with."

"O.K. Call the first witness," Judge Spud Berkley ordered.

Helen tried for composure but dissolved again into tears when she started recounting the horrible crime.

"Mr. Greyco, what do you have to say for yourself?" I asked him.

Greyco walked over to Cecil and rubbed against the leg of his overall.

"Get away from me," Cecil said roughly, even as his hand unconsciously went down to rub him.

"Your honor," I looked at the defendant. "Greyco was caught red-handed. As Papa would say, it's an open and shut case. Let the law take its course." I'll bet that was the most honest and the shortest plea any defense attorney has ever made.

"Attorney 'Winkie' Berkley, you may talk." Winkie was a pet name we sometimes called Cecil.

Cecil who had refused to defend Greyco, also refused to prosecute. He made a much better defense for him than I did.

"Your honor, we know little Cora got killed this morning. Greyco musta done it 'cause when we came up he was standin' over her. He didn't say he did, he didn't say he didn't. Your honor, Greyco didn't say nothing. No matter what we do it ain't gonna bring Cora back. I ask the court to run him out of town," Cecil finished his plea weakly.

"What he's done is too bad to let go. 'Spose he was run outa this town. He might go to another town an' do the same thing. I order you, Greyco, to hang for the murder of Cora." Then as an afterthought Spud added, " 'N may the Lord have mercy on your soul."

Spud shed his role of justice quickly and ran to the barn, coming back with a long piece of rope. He was now chief executioner.

Making a slip knot in one end, he tried to throw the other end over the branch of an apple tree. Finally he shimmied up the tree with the rope and put it over the limb. He slid down and reached for Greyco who was still following us about as though we were his best friends.

"Now hold on to the other end, Cecil," Spud yelled. "And don't you let go," he cautioned. Helen and I stood close together out of the way. Helen's eyes were bright with excitement.

"Do you think we ought to?" she whispered to me.

"Sure," was my weak answer.

It all happened as quickly as the wink of a lightning bug in August. One minute Spud had Greyco in his arms, carefully pulling the rope tighter and tighter about his throat. The next minute the other end of the rope was securely fastened around the slender trunk of the June-apple tree and Greyco's lithe body was turning flips in the air. For a second he would be still; then he would start again. The whining was muffled but the effort to escape was vigorous.

"Better let him down now, Spud. I think he's dead," Cecil advised.

"Naw, he ain't." Spud was determined to see justice done.

"Well, anyway, he's dying. Let him down so he can die on the ground."

"He ain't near dead. You know a cat got nine lives. He ain't got rid of but three of 'em yet." Spud was trying to be stout-hearted but we could see he was weakening.

Any child is very receptive to sign language. After he grows up he needs to use a lot of words to be understood. I nodded toward the rope that was tied to the tree trunk, then to Spud. In no time at all Cecil was bearing Spud to earth with a weak half nelson around his neck, and I was untying the rope from the tree. Greyco slid towards the ground, clawing the air.

"I'll let you up if you'll take that rope offa Greyco's neck," Cecil panted.

"Heck, I wasn't gonna let 'em die, nohow. I just wanted to teach him a lesson. Bet he won't eat no more little chickens."

Spud got up. Automatically he brushed his trousers as he walked quickly over to where Greyco strained at the rope. He loosened the rope and like a shot Greyco lit out through the grape arbor, over the back field, and when last we saw him he was speeding across the race track.

That evening after dinner Mother stood in the doorway with a plate of tempting cat food.

"Kitty, Kitty," she called. She waited for a few minutes, then set the dish down on the floor.

The next morning the food was still there. As we were eating breakfast, Mother remarked about it.

"Wonder what's the matter with that fool cat? Never touched his supper last night."

"You know, Mama," Helen came to our rescue, "when he first came here, you said he was a rambler, and wouldn't stay in one place long. Maybe he rambled on away."

"Maybe so." Mother thought for a while, then took the dish off the floor, scraped the food in the garbage pail, and sighed, "But do you know I was really getting fond of that critter."

There was no time that morning to pay our last respects to Cora. We had spent too much time prosecuting the offender. Besides, Cora was such a neighborhood favorite we wanted all our playmates to attend the funeral.

Cecil had put little Cora in a small shoe box. From my

doll things I found a piece of yellow silk, just the color of Cora's soft feathers. We covered her with the silk, put the top on the box, and set it upon a high shelf in the smoke-house.

Spud and Cecil were out of school a half hour before we were. When we reached home they had the shallow grave dug and the little pasteboard coffin sitting on another small box. We noticed that Cora's grave was not to be in the regular chicken graveyard. We had a plot of ground over near the barn where all the chickens, who just laid down and died without having their necks wrung off, were buried. Cora's grave was underneath the cherry tree in the garden.

"We didn't put her with the ordinary chickens," Cecil pointed out.

"Well, we didn't know them as well as we did Cora," Spud explained.

"It'll be pretty over Cora's grave when the cherry tree blooms in the spring. I'm glad you did it." Helen was always quick to praise.

Soon there were about fifteen kids in the yard. There was no yelling or pushing or good-natured fun. Nellie and Ernest Sadberry came from across the road. Yeets and Anna Molsen, Hans and Willie Tutos, Polish youngsters from the next block, Katherine Warren, Herschel and Willie Stevenson, were joined by Orlean and Ernestine, our two cousins from the North End.

Spud was the preacher. Helen, Cecil, and Nellie Sadberry were the chief mourners. They could all cry at will. I directed the choir composed of Orlean, Ernestine, and Willie Stevenson. The rest were just interested spectators.

We opened the services by singing "Nearer, My God to Thee." Soon we were joined by another voice. I paused to listen. Herschel Stevenson, with his big head thrown back was singing loudly, "Nero, my dog got fleas, Nero got fleas."

He was silenced by the look of disapproval on each serious young face. We only knew one verse of the song; so as soon as it was finished Spud stood up and began his sermon.

"We are gathered here, sisters and brothers, to pay the last token of respect to this, our deceased sister. Cora was a sweet soul. She never done a thing to make anybody unhappy, but as the Bible says, the good die young. Thas what happened to Cora. You will all miss Cora."

"Yes," Helen wailed. Nellie was also sniffling by this time.

"When you go out in the yard, Cora won't be following you around."

"No," Helen sanctioned.

"When you go in the house, you won't be seeing her. When you get to the supper table there'll be one vacant chair. Maybe you'll look in the closet. Her clothes will be hanging up there, but Cora will be gone."

Something that sounded like a snicker came from the Polish part of the congregation. Again we frowned our disapproval and taking their cue from our serious faces, Anna, Yeets, Willie, and Hans also put on woebegone expressions.

"As I said before, Cora never harmed a hair on nobody's head—yet death struck her down."

"Amen!" Willie Stevenson shouted.

"You don't know the day or the hour when death will come riding by on his pale white horse and say, 'Come on in. You done hoed your row out.' Will you be ready? Thas the main question. Will you be papaired when Gab'iel will step down over the battlements of glory, put that silver trumpet to his lips, and blo-o-ow time into eternity?"

Spud, now thoroughly lost in his flow of oratory, was

preaching almost word for word the funeral sermon of Rev. Barner. We knew it was make-believe but somehow we were trapped by the backwash of emotion. I was suddenly afflicted with throat trouble. A lump as big as a hen egg wouldn't come up or go down. Anna Molsen was crying with Helen and Nellie. Two or three of the boys brushed their eyes quickly. Spud stopped his sermon abruptly, nodded to me and sat down.

"We will sing, 'In the Sweet Bye and Bye,' " I announced.

> There's a land that is fairer than day,
> And by faith we can see——

No one was singing. Orlean and Ernestine had dissolved into tears. Spud, always equal to the occasion, took the little box and placed it in the grave.

"Dust to dust," he chanted. I sprinkled a handful of dirt over the top of the box. "Ashes to ashes, and earth to earth."

Slowly we pushed the little mound of dirt over the box.

"Poor little Cora," Cecil murmured softly.

"She'll be a long time gone, won't she?" Willie Stevenson said solemnly.

"Yes," I tried to clear my throat. "Yes, she'll be a long time gone."

10. and may the best man win

Our family couldn't be a house divided against itself—that is, outwardly. At home there might be heated arguments as to the relative merits of this or that candidate, but everybody knew that all the Berkleys would march to the polls in one body and vote the straight Republican ticket.

"You vote the way you want and I'll do the same. Geeminy! I'm grown, Braxton," Uncle Bob would yell in his high-pitched voice. Uncle Bob was Dad's younger brother but they were as alike as twins.

"I know you're grown but you're acting like a child. Letting Homer McGee and Bert Wilson lead you around like they got a ring in your nose." Dad's voice had an edge on it, too.

"I ain't been listening to Homer McGee or Bert Wilson. I can think for myself. That's something you don't want me to do."

"Now Robert, you listen to Buddy," Aunt Ida essayed the role of arbitrator. "He's been in the game a long time. He never steered you wrong."

"Not much!" Uncle Bob's huff was a cross between a grunt and a short bitter laugh. "Didn't he tell us to put Rowan Tinsley in the state House? You remember, Braxton, you remember!" His right forefinger wriggled accusingly two inches from Dad's nose. "He was running against Albert Grainger, and what did Tinsley do?"

"Well," Dad conceded weakly, "he wasn't the man I thought he was."

"Wasn't the man you thought he was? He wasn't no man at all. The operators bought him off. Every time one of our bills come up, Tinsley was off fishing."

Dad had always smarted under that double cross, but he couldn't back down now. A man was entitled to one mistake. Everybody made mistakes. That's why they put erasers on lead pencils. And Dad would certainly redeem himself by blotting out little Rowan Tinsley's political star.

When election for state assemblyman rolled around again, Rowan was sure of the miners. He dropped by the house rather casually to assure himself of Dad's support.

"Well, Mr. Berkley, it should be a landslide this time," he smiled broadly.

"It will be," Dad paused, then added significantly, "for Albert Grainger."

Dad seldom joked when talking business and Rowan Tinsley knew this. The ingratiating smile left his face but his voice held the same high hopefulness.

"He won't be any trouble. I'll admit it was a pretty close race last time, but with my record——"

"That's just what's going to kill you, Tinsley," Dad interrupted, "your record."

"Why, Mr. Berkley, I don't understand. What was wrong with my record?"

"It ain't no need to beat the devil around the stump, Tinsley. Look! We elected you to work for the miners. You didn't have no money to run your campaign. All right. We won't work for money. You had been a good district attorney. You'd been fair. We liked you. We believed in you. The other side waved a thousand dollar bill under my nose.

I spit on it. A thousand dollars is a whole lot of money, Tinsley. 'Specially for the little work I'd a had to do to elect Grainger. I know politics, Tinsley. I was in this game when you was still wearing didies. I ain't no mealy-mouthed hat-in-my-hand politician. I ain't like one of these bread-and-butter preachers who'll promise to vote their congregation to a man if you'll come over to their church dinners and buy up all the grub. I'm president of the Stand Patters' Club. We run the Second Ward. I ain't bragging. I'm stating a cold fact. I run the Second Ward—and the Second Ward runs this town."

"I know that, Mr. Berkley. I know that. But I'm telling you the God's truth. I thought I voted the way you boys wanted me to vote."

"When you was there," Dad agreed. "But the times you wasn't there was the most important. And another thing, don't talk about—us boys. I'm old enough for your daddy, though if I thought any one of my boys would be a sneaking dirty sellout like you—I'd a drowned him when he was born."

All pompousness had gone. Tinsley's feigned innocence had failed. Being a good lawyer, he now resorted to persuasion.

"Mr. Berkley, you can't let me down. I'm white, you're black, but we're both poor and we poor folks have to stick together. Grainger is from the East Side. You know whose interest he will foster. I grew up on the West Side. I've always fought for our own people. Honest to God, I have."

"Leave God's name out of it, Tinsley. You ain't the man I thought you was. I wouldn't believe you if you swore on a stack of Bibles as high as this house. You're through. You

98

done dug your own grave. You better crawl in and pull the dirt over you."

"But you can't desert me, Uncle Brack." Tinsley was using every trick, even to calling Dad by the special name only his closest young intimates used.

"I didn't desert you. You deserted us. I'm warning you, Tinsley, if the other side give you any money you'd sure better hold on to it. It's gonna have to last you a long time. You didn't know who you was fooling with. You done got too big for your pants. A bird can fly high but he got to come down to the ground to eat. You're done—washed up and washed out. If you got a trump card, you sure better play it. You'll find out before you're many days older that a cow needs her tail more than once in fly time."

Rowan Tinsley walked like an old man as he went back up Walnut Street.

"Ain't no need of you bringing that up, Robert. I wasn't by myself. Wasn't nothing wrong with Tinsley at first, but a little money can change a man's mind. Tinsley was just weak, but a weak man don't fill the bill. This time Grainger is the man. You say you was for him at first. Then what changed you? How much are Homer McGee and Bert Wilson paying for votes—a can of beer?"

"Robert, you ought to work with Buddy. Dad always said that we should stick together." Aunt Ida was gentle, but insistent.

"All right. All right. Braxton is the Lord God. He's always right. It's always what he says, or nothing." Uncle Bob was weakening, but not gracefully.

"Now Robert, don't take the Lord's name in vain," Aunt Ida admonished. "Buddy's been like a father to us since Dad went away."

"I guess me and Braxton understand each other," Uncle Bob looked at Dad. A truce had been declared. Again they were on the same side. They went up the street and were soon talking and joking with the men in front of John Simmons' pool hall.

Dad had a sixth sense for judging men. Seldom was he deceived. Even when he was being flattered, and Dad was a sucker for flattery, he usually saw through the scheme while his chest was swelling with pride. The flatterer was never an out-and-out rascal. He was a good boy, but just weak.

Dad never took a course in child psychology. Maybe it was just as well, for the Berkley method certainly met with our approval. Children are natural hero-worshippers, and Dad was the object of our undivided adoration. We were never thrilled by the exploits of Babe Ruth. Wouldn't Dad stand up by Aunt Ida's house and knock a ball over into the middle of ole man Wench's field before the neighborhood baseball game was over?

As children, we saw nothing profound in the choice bits of homespun logic and bits of advice that came spontaneously from Dad's lips as we sat about the supper table or ate parched field corn about the big base-burner at night. We trusted him implicitly, and judging from the many types of people who came to our house to see him, many others shared our faith.

A rap at the door could mean anything, from a pimp who wanted his prostitute sprung from the local bastille, to Governor Deneen, on vacation from the state capitol, who wanted to borrow Prince and Blizzard, Dad's prize bird dogs, for a day's hunting in the woods near Beauchoup Bottoms. We soon learned to respect all human beings, disregarding such exterior trappings as clothing, color, or speech.

We were bugging Irish potatoes one evening when we looked across the field and saw District Attorney Albert Grainger coming over the footbridge that spanned a small creek that flowed through our place. He was a tall, good-looking, Vincent Price sort of a fellow with ruddy complexion and wavy brown hair.

"Lookee, Papa," Spud pointed at the man striding down the long rows. "Here comes somebody."

"I guess he knows where he's going." Dad flipped a big yellow and black potato bug into the tin can which held coal oil.

"Hello there, Mr. Berkley," the man called when he got within hailing distance.

"Good evening, sir," Dad called back.

Soon they were shaking hands.

"Attorney Grainger, I'd like my children to know you. This is Helen; this is Ruby, sometimes I call her Reuben," he hugged me to him affectionately. "This one is little Brack and this here is Cecil."

"A fine bunch of youngsters, Mr. Berkley. I see you're bringing them up right. Teaching them to share the responsibility of the home. It's a fine idea. I've seen the boys down around the New Merchant Hotel."

"I 'speck you have. Brack and Cecil get the garbage from the kitchen there. A hog can grow on it, but I always feed them ship stuff and corn to make the meat sweet and the fat solid."

"I see you know what to do to have good meat for the winter. Mr. Berkley, I wanted to talk to you. I see you're busy but if you could spare me a few minutes——"

"We always take time to do what we want to do, Mr. Grainger," Dad smiled and set his half-filled can of bugs down.

"I'm glad to hear you say that. I know it's early to be thinking of general elections, but past experience has taught me that you can't begin planting too soon, and I thought——"

"Let's go over here by the fence," Dad suggested. When they were almost out of earshot he added with a laugh, "These younguns are at the stage where they are all stomach and ears."

The fence divided Grandpa Berkley's holdings from the huge acreage commonly known as Horn's pasture which belonged to Henry Horn. We could tell by the way Dad used his hands and his head that the conversation was important. At times his lips were compressed in a hard straight line and he would shake his head vigorously. At other times his head bobbed in approval like a wound-up mechanical toy.

With Dad, the pace setter away from the job, Spud and Cecil began to loaf on the job. They played tag, jumping over the plants. Although deep in conversation with Attorney Grainger, Dad kept an eye on us. Humor lay lightly beneath his sternness, for he called out to Spud and Cecil:

Boys, oh boys, give the poor Irish potatoes a chance;
For you know in the morning, you can't find your pants.

Lawyer Grainger laughed heartily. Helen and I snickered as the boys went earnestly back to work. It was a well-known fact around our house that no matter where Spud and Cecil put their clothing when they pulled them off at night, they were always sure to need assistance in finding them the next morning.

Twilight lingers long on the prairie. We finished our rows, gathered up our cans and sticks, and started back to the house well ahead of Dad and Mr. Grainger. Later Dad gave us the following political advice: "Never approach a candidate first. When you ask a man a favor, you put yourself at his mercy; when he asks a favor of you, the power is on your side."

As election time drew near, Dad's actions became increasingly strange. Mother and Aunt Ida discussed it as they tackled a basket of mending.

"Sophia, what's come over Buddy, this election?"

"I don't know, Ida. It's not like Braxton to stay out of the game. Why, ever since we've been married he's had the Stand Patters' Club and they usually elect their men."

"I know." Aunt Ida was puzzled. "Dad thinks that Homer McGee and Bert Wilson scared Buddy out. They made their brags that anybody Buddy was for they would work against.

"I've never known Braxton to back down because he was scared of anybody. He hasn't said who he is for. He went to the church supper the other night. Rowan Tinsley was there buying chicken dinners for all the folks."

"I saw him. He was real friendly to Tinsley, too. I can't understand it."

"Me, neither. I don't think he'd work for Tinsley again. Not after what he told him right here in this room."

"It ain't natural for Buddy not to take part. I asked him point-blank the other day who he was going to vote for."

"What did he tell you?"

"Said he wasn't sure."

"Just goes to show you, you never know a man. Ida, I've been married to Braxton for years. Every other election he's charged up like a fire horse when he hears the whistle. This time he doesn't even wear a button. Won't talk election at all. Just says the only candidate he's interested in is George Smith for constable, and nobody has run against George since God knows when."

For a while, Aunt Ida and Mama sewed in silence.

Dad had two mortal enemies—Homer McGee and Bert Wilson. Homer McGee was a newcomer who had ridden into town on a wave of glory. He was a union organizer. That he had been so successful in Du Quoin was not due to any organizational genius on his part. The pasture was not as virgin as it may have looked. While operators, with the aid of the local police declared open season on organizers in most towns, Du Quoin's first union under the supervision of Peter Kauffman, W. T. Mitchell, and Dad steadily and rapidly grew from a rather secretive house-to-house gathering, into Local No. 98 with over 1100 active members.

On the records of the national organization Homer McGee's name meant the same as Joel Kupperman's on a quiz kid show. It was a terrible disappointment to them when Homer, after dodging two bullets in Jackson County, gave up organizing and came back to Du Quoin to live the safe and peaceful life of an ordinary coal digger.

A few of the younger miners who did not know the actual birth pangs of the local, worshipped Homer as a brave and fearless leader. The older ones, remembering the risks they had taken and the insecurity they faced, had their labor affiliations become known too soon, labeled him as a braggart and accused Homer of ignoring the bridge that carried him over.

Dad blamed himself for Bert Wilson's enmity.

"That Bert is a queer fellow," Ernest Smith said the day

before the election as he and Dad discussed some of the townspeople. "When he came here he was so ragged he had to carry his money in his mouth. You let him stay with you and Sophia until he could get on his feet. Stood for him to get some clothes from the company store, got him a job in the mines. You done everything for him, Unca Brack. Now the worse thing he can say about you is too good. He's Homer McGee's right hand man now. That's gratitude."

"Ernest," Dad said solemnly, "never make the mistake of taking care of a grown person that ain't sick, and then expect him to appreciate it. If a man is satisfied in a ditch, leave him there. Of course, if he's struggling to get out, give him a helping hand. Nobody thanks you for making them beholding to you. Nobody thanks you for making him a beggar. He may ask you to do it, may beg you to do it, but when you do, just bend over for a swift kick in the backsides. It's sure to come."

Election day Dad was up early and on his way to the mines with his dinner pail. This was as unorthodox as going to the mines on the first day of quail season. It just wasn't done. Dad passed around the corner of the house and out across the road to catch the "coaches" that were to take the men to the mines. He was singing gaily and I snuggled deeper into the covers as I listened to his voice growing fainter and fainter:

> Then let us rise, shine,
> Give God the glory, glory,
> Rise, shine, give God the glory,
> Soldiers of the cross.

All day Homer McGee and Bert Wilson drove about the city in the shiny surreys from Maclin's stables. Occasionally they touched a whip to the spirited bays, or gallantly lifted their Derby hats to passing ladies.

Dad came from the mines about four o'clock. We knew there was something in the air by the way he rushed into the house, scrubbed himself hurriedly in the large zinc tub, gulped his food, and hotfooted it off for town.

"Braxton," Dad called to Spud as he started down the street, "run over on Smoke Row and tell Aunt Frankie Woods and Aunt Tishie Sampson to get ready to go to the polls. I'll be 'round for them in a few minutes."

"But Braxton," Mother yelled after him, "Homer McGee and Bert Wilson been voting people all day."

"Bet they didn't vote none of mine." The ring of a conqueror was in Dad's voice.

"But you never told us how to vote. Ida and I didn't know."

"For God's sake, woman, I ain't got time to stand here talking all day. The polls close at six o'clock. Get ready! I'll be back after you!"

We looked at Mother, thinking to see a hurt expression at the harshness of Dad's voice. Instead, a slow smile crinkled the corners of her mouth and her eyes were bright with affectionate pride.

"Ruby, you better run tell Ida and Dea that we're going to the polls as soon as Braxton gets back." She entered the house, untied her gingham apron, threw it over the back of a kitchen chair, and passed on into the bedroom to change her dress.

"Look at the parade coming down the street!" Cecil yelled as he took his eyes off the large ring of marbles and glanced up Walnut Street.

"Ain't no parade——". Spud squinted his left eye and knuckled down to shoot.

" 'Tis too," Cecil insisted.

Spud's prize agate still rested between his thumb and forefinger. He looked up the street and became as excited as Cecil as he watched the procession coming down South Walnut. Dad clucked to a midnight-black horse that pulled a phaeton over the bumpy dirt roads. Behind him came Freeman Sampson's nephew, young Rob Jenkins, driving a pair of roans, Riley Lane maneuvered two nervous sorrels, and little Jerome Jackson, not yet old enough to vote but who worshipped Dad in the place of a father he had not known, drove a dapple-gray team. Never had we seen so many shiny carriages coming down Walnut Street, unless there was a funeral. At the corner of South Street and Walnut the drivers went in several directions.

"Mama, Mama," Spud called, "here comes Papa driving Jake Druer's horse, Midnight."

"Tell him I'll be out in a minute."

"Mama said she'd be out in a minute," Cecil delivered the message for Spud was too awed by the beauty of the big black horse to remember what Mother had said.

"Tell her not to make her minute too long."

Before Cecil could repeat Dad's words, Mother came out the door with an uneven smear of powder across her right cheek, her hair combed high and rolled on one side.

"Get some of that flour off your face before you get in this buggy with me." Dad's voice was stern but his eyes were laughing.

"What did Aunt Frankie Woods and Aunt Tishie say? Did Aunt George Ann vote today?" Mother questioned Dad, as she rubbed her fingers over her cheek.

"Just what they'd say to anybody if they knowed I didn't send 'em." Dad laughed. ("Ah wouldn't move two feet away from mah snuff can to go nowhere unless Braxton told me how to vote," they told McGee and Wilson. "What do Ah know 'bout you strange niggers?")

Ten minutes before the polls closed, Dad and his henchmen had voted their last man. The Stand Patters' Club, which had announced its disbanding months before the election, had miraculously come to life.

"Homer McGee and Bert Wilson sure made themselves scarce when Braxton showed up." Ernest Smith grinned as he thought of the eventful day. It was nearly midnight when the votes were all counted. The men still crowded Joe Knapp's saloon and rehashed the most exciting day in the history of Ward Number Two. The room grew quiet as McGee and Wilson pushed open the swinging doors. They looked about, and came slowly over to Dad's table.

"Mr. Grainger told us to see you," Homer McGee was the spokesman.

"I don't see what for. I've paid off all the men I hired to work in the election." Dad was enjoying their discomfort.

"Grainger hired us."

"Then get your money from him." Dad ignored the two men and yelled to Slim behind the counter, "Bring me my bill, Slim."

"We went to him but he said you were paying off in the Second Ward."

"But you couldn'ta been working for Grainger. You said before the election came up that you'd work against anybody I worked for. You musta been working for Rowan Tinsley. What did Attorney Grainger tell you?"

"He said, you boys find Mr. Berkley. He's managed my

campaign and I know he'll treat you right," Bert Wilson repeated the attorney's words.

"But, Bert, I can't do anything for you and Homer. You was out to beat me. You told Grainger that I didn't have no influence. I was just a bluff. You can't want to do any business with me."

"We want what we worked for," McGee said doggedly.

Dad took a large roll of bills from his pocket, peeled off two twenties and a ten and laid them on the table.

"Scornful dogs'll eat dirty pudding," he remarked to Rob Jenkins.

McGee and Wilson snatched for the bills and hurried through the side door, not turning to see who had started the roar of derisive laughter that followed them out into the dark street.

11. carnival time

Twice a year the town awoke to the lumbering of heavy wagons over the ruts in the dirt road. For weeks now, we had stood entranced before the flaming posters that covered the sides of the downtown store buildings and the barns.

By no stretch of the imagination could heaven be as beautiful and exciting as the jostling midway of a carnival. We were the luckiest kids in town for we lived only half a block from the carnival grounds, and we could stand in our own field and watch the horses run on the track behind our house. Nobody had to be called twice on the morning the carnival rolled into town.

"My goodness," Mother exclaimed as we hurriedly gathered our books for school. "Aren't you children getting out a little early? Look at all the food you've wasted. There are many children in this world who would be glad to get such a nice breakfast."

And it was nice. There were thick slices of home-cured ham, fluffy hot biscuits, small servings of delicious home-canned yellow cling peaches, and rich milk from Cherry, our Holstein cow. By ten o'clock, we would be hungry enough to eat boiled sawdust. Now our only thought was to get over to the carnival ground and see what was going up.

Helen, Cecil, and I left Spud looking for his cap. Spud was always looking for his cap. He could come home to lunch with it safely perched on his long head but he'd usually enter the house giving a good imitation of the war whoop of a Comanche Indian, sail his cap toward the first chair, and spring for the table. No matter where he put his cap, he always had to hunt for it. This morning was no exception. We were half way down the block when Spud caught and passed us. Our pace was much too slow for him. Near the corner we met Bessie, Nellie, and Ernest Sadberry.

Bessie's face had a few becoming freckles, and she wore her hair in two long braids. Nellie was shy, but we liked her because she didn't cry much. Ernest was a rather lanky, good-looking, brown-skinned boy, but his nose had an awful habit of running a great part of the time.

"Hi," we greeted each other. We were soon joined by Luther Clary and "Dollar Bill" Roberts, unopposed leaders of the south end gang.

"Is it a big carnival?" we asked excitedly. Somehow, we knew that Luther and Dollar Bill had all the answers.

"Big? Why, it would make three of that little ole dinky one that was here last year," Dollar Bill bragged.

"Naw!" Cecil's voice was filled with awe. He was always easily impressed.

All my life I've tried to be a skeptic, so I said coldly, "How do you know?"

"He wouldn'ta if it hadna been for me," Luther informed us. "The carnival got in town about five o'clock this morning. I got up, dressed, and laid the fire in the kitchen stove for Ma. Then I sneaked out and went over to Dollar Bill's house to wake him up. If his window hadna been up, I never woulda woke him. I've heard some fancy snoring in my day, but ole Dollar sure was tackin' 'em down this morning."

"Gwan, Luther. You stretchin' it some." Dollar nudged Luther playfully.

"I ain't neither. If I snored as loud as you, I never would get no sleep, 'cause everytime I'd go to sleep, I'd wake my own self up." We all laughed.

Luther was our local John Henry. He was a strong, black boy with wide shoulders, a right arm that packed a mean backhand lick, and a set of teeth that were formed out of mother-of-pearl. He could outfight, outrun, outwork any boy in the south end of town. He never used his strength to terrorize. He minded his own business. He hated bullies, and because all the kids in town respected him, we were glad to have him for our friend.

Now we turned the corner, and right before our eyes a huge fairyland was being created. Some of the men in their dirty shirt sleeves lugged heavy boxes. As others pulled and strained at the strong hemp ropes, large canvas flaps billowed out like huge sails on an ancient frigate. The foreman spiked every order with good-natured profanity. Wives of the showmen, looking tired and pale in the clear sharp spring air, sat on boxes near their half-erected concessions and rubbed the sleep from their eyes. Two or three girls from the *Streets of Paris* show, without make-up and with frowzy hair, walked uncertainly in their thin shoes with corkscrew heels over toward the hamburger wagon. The untidy cook wore a chef's cap and a dirty apron that served as a hand-towel most of the time. The small patties of uncooked meat were not as red as the hamburgers our Mary and Henry Fritz sold customers over their shining, white-enamel counter. The meat looked anemic, but once mashed out and laid on the hot, greasy grill, it sent forth the most delicious smell in the world.

"Um-m-m." We drew in deep breaths.

The five-minute bell from Lincoln School yanked us back to the dusty streets of Du Quoin with their weather-boarded, weather-beaten houses.

"Let's get going. We gonna be late," Helen admonished.

We raced toward the two-story, brick building where Mrs. Anderson and Miss Emma Tate stood on the steps with Isis-like eyes watching the children line up to march into the temple of knowledge.

Running is such good fun when you are young and happy. The scent of strong, black coffee, hamburgers, and onion was still in our nostrils. We did not hear Philip Sousa's "Under the Double Eagle" coming from the metallic victrola that stood on the first landing. We could still hear the pleasant voice of the carnival man, who called to us as we sprinted toward school, "See you kids tonight."

Nothing short of death could have kept us from the carnival ground that night. Like a magic potion brewed by the hand of Hippocrates, its enchantment had the power to heal the sick and make the lame walk. After school we went past the grounds again. Some of the older boys were permitted to work at last-minute tasks. The ferris wheel was already filled with grinning youngsters who held their breath and drew up their shoulders every time the large wheel dropped them toward the earth. From the merry-go-round, or the flying Jenny, as the old folks called it, the melody of "Pretty Baby," the current hit tune, sounded throughout the midway. Now it came to a stop, and the youngsters raced to climb upon their favorite plaster-cast steed with flying mane and tail.

Watching others ride wasn't too much fun; so we walked slowly home. We left Dollar Bill, Luther, and Ernest at the carnival working for spending money. Grace Cantloe walked along with us, swinging her books.

"Coming early?" she inquired.

"Just as soon as supper's over," Helen answered.

"How much you gonna spend?" Grace wanted to know.

"Oh, Dad will give us a quarter apiece," I spoke up proudly.

"Bess, le's ask Papa for a quarter, too," Nellie suggested.

"A quarter?" I hated Grace's superior laugh. She had come from East St. Louis. Aunt Dea said one day that East St. Louis was a hellhole, but Grace made it sound big and wonderful. London or New York must be something like East St. Louis, we reasoned. "You can't do nothing with a quarter. J. T.'s gonna give me a dollar to spend."

J. T. was her stepfather, but we thought it sacrilege to call any older person by his first name.

"A dollar?" I wanted to be sure I heard aright.

"Yes, Legs," she informed me. She had used the unglamorous name I was sometimes called by. If I liked you, you could call me anything—almost, but I didn't like Grace.

"A dollar," I shrugged my shoulders. "He better take it and pay his grocery bill at Forester's store. I heard Eddley Thornton tell him the other day that he wasn't going to let him have another thing 'til he straightened up his account."

"Ruby!" Helen was mortified.

"Well, it's true. That's what he said. I was standing right by the window. I don't have to story."

"Wait 'til I tell Mama," Helen threatened.

"I don't care." I had defeated the adversary, or, to be more explicit, I had stopped the lion's mouth, for Grace, taking advantage of Helen's interference, had crossed the street and was hurrying toward her home.

Old people will never be able to understand children. I remember how slowly Mama and Dad moved about the house that evening; how meticulously Mother served supper, insisting on a just rightness that exasperated us to distraction. Day wanted to tarry forever, but night finally limped in.

The midway was filled with people. Bright-eyed youngsters tethered to the seamy hands of their elders, tugged to break free and go exploring under their own steam. Under the bright lights, the old patched tents, the frayed banners with their worn-off paintings, the booths were as gay as a Sultan's bazaar. A barker stood before the *Streets of Paris*.

"Right this way, folks; right this way. See the most beautiful girls in the world. Every one a star. Every one the acme of feminine pulchritude. Every one of these gorgeous beauties here for your special entertainment. If you want a good time, if you are still looking for something to give you a thrill, buy your ticket and step right in. The *Streets of Paris* is new—it's exciting," and here his voice dropped to a sibilant whisper that carried to the edge of the crowd, "it's naughty! Step right up, men, get your tickets. One dime, the tenth part of a dollar, just two nickels, folks. A dime—ten cents."

A small band near the entrance started playing "Everybody's Doing It." The girls in their expertly applied drugstore complexions, switched off the platform and were assisted down the short ladder. For a few seconds they hovered near the entrance. They smiled bewitchingly, then disappeared behind the flap of the tent as a crowd of men stampeded over the platform.

With just a little money to spend, one either becomes a fool or a shrewd bargainer. Within half an hour, we had sized up all the concessions and had figured out the ones that offered the greatest odds and the least. We knew we would find Dad at the shooting gallery, for he was a crack shot. When we reached there, Dad and the man who ran the concession were in an argument.

"Don't tell me," Dad shouted. "Either the barrel's crooked or this sight is off."

"Why don't you admit you're no William Tell," the man joked. "Be a good sport, have another try. It's only a dime."

"Gimme another gun," Dad said gruffly.

"Here you are, mister. Now take your time. Easy— e-e-easy," the man sounded like he was talking to a nervous horse. I wanted to warn the man, but a crowd of people had gathered around the booth. Evidently he was one of our misguided tragedians who thinks he is court jester.

Dad watched the little ducks as they were carried across the racks.

"This'll be duck soup for Dad," I whispered to Cecil.

Dad now had the gun to his shoulder. He pressed the trigger. Nothing happened. Again Dad fired. The little ducks sailed serenely on. Dad fired a third time.

"Aha! Our local William Tell has missed again."

"Listen." Dad's voice was deadly serious. "I don't know nothing about this here William Tell, but I do know how to shoot. Last year I broke ninety-seven clay pigeons out of a hundred, and they wasn't travelin' in a straight line. This season I got the limit of quails every time I went out, some- times I got more than that, but I give 'em to the other boys so it wouldn't look bad if the game warden got curious. I don't care which way them ducks was travelin'; if your guns was right, I could hit 'em."

"You want to ruin my business. You want to say my game is crooked."

"It is."

"Don't you call me a liar. I won't take that off no n——"

"Jes say it," Dad challenged, "Jes say it, and you'll find yourself gettin' up from behind that row o' ducks."

"You'd better get on away from here, or I'll call a cop."

"Charlie Layman's as scared of me as you are. Don't worry, you'll make money. There's a sucker born every minute, they say."

It was almost nine o'clock and time to go home when we found Spud. He was standing before a bare-looking concession. Three small kegs were mounted on slightly tilted platforms. A row of hams and sides of bacon were strung across the rack near the front. Several people were standing nearby.

"Anybody can win, folks, anybody can win. Just throw three little balls in these three great big barrels. Take home a nice juicy ham or a thick side of bacon. Step right up, folks; don't be afraid to try your luck. Three balls for a quarter. It costs so little to win so much."

The singsong voice of the man brought no flurry of customers.

"Come on folks. It's not every day you can get a whole ham for a quarter. Three balls for just a quarter, folks. Step right up and try your luck."

"A quarter's pretty high," Charlie Warren, whom we called Big Head, yelled out from the crowd. "I won this with a dime." He held up a rosy-cheeked kewpie doll. Nearly everybody had one. Charlie failed to mention that he had spent nearly three dollars trying to win a watch by throwing hoops over a square, velvet-covered box. A twenty-five cent chalk doll, that would break if you looked at her too hard, had been his only premium.

"Step closer, buddy," the man beckoned to Charlie. His voice dropped to an intimate whisper. "A good salesman never knocks another man's goods, see. Live and let live is my motto. All right. You spent a dime, didn't you?"

"That's what I said."

"Maybe you spent more than that. Maybe you spent four bits or a dollar?" Charlie was noncommittal. "I ain't saying for sure you did, I said—maybe," the man reminded him.

"Well, maybe," Charlie admitted grudgingly.

"Understand me now," the man's voice dropped even lower, "as I said at first, I ain't knocking nobody. Every fellow to his notion as a monkey to his motion, but I'm asking you for the truth. Now after all your time and money —what have you got? Just a pretty trinket," he answered himself. "Something to catch the eye, but nothing to tickle your palate. For two bits, just think of it, for a measly quarter you can eat ham for a week."

Attracted by the man's glib talk and intrigued by the nuances in his voice, many people had crowded around the stand. Charlie, who stood six feet two, towered over most of them. He swallowed hard and looked down at Bertha, a petite brunette who stood at his side.

"Go on, Big Head," she said, calling Charlie by his nickname.

"Come on," the man encouraged. Now his voice was filled with wonderment. "Look at that arm, folks. Buddy, where did you get that arm? Did you get it pitching for the Giants?"

"No. Swinging a pick at Majestic mines," Charlie answered proudly.

All the while the fellow talked, he held the three balls in his hand. Now he shoved them into Charlie's hand and motioned the crowd back. "Give him plenty of room, folks. Watch him win. What are you going to take, mister, a ham or a side of bacon?"

Charlie was completely sold. He gave the man a quarter, then threw one of the balls into the air to judge its weight. Several others laid their quarters on the counter and awaited their turns.

Charlie's first ball landed in a barrel. Then, out it popped and rolled over to the side in the sawdust.

"Too much spring in it, buddy. Put 'em in and make 'em stay in," the man cautioned good-naturedly. The last two balls met a similar fate.

The other men tried, but they were no more successful than Charlie. A part of the crowd started to move on. The sharpster tried another line of attack. He always had an ace in the hole.

"Stand up here, sonny," he addressed a small boy standing near the front who had been completely hidden in the crowd. The boy hopped up on the counter.

"Gee, it's Spud!" I whispered.

"Golly!" Cecil was as awed as I was. Remembering the time Spud had volunteered for a hypnotic experiment at Zion Methodist Church, we didn't know what was going to happen, but knowing Spud, we knew he was game for anything. We remembered how Uncle Robert had marched up to the platform and yanked Spud out of the chair just as Professor Nedwilly began to chant some mumbo jumbo and make a few passes in front of Spud's face.

We looked about with expectation hoping that Uncle Robert would again intervene. He was nowhere to be seen.

"I'm going to find Dad," Cecil whispered and slithered off through the crowd.

"Show them what you won, sonny," the man smiled benignly at the small dark brown boy in faded overalls.

Spud smiled, displaying an uneven long tooth in front. Great day in the morning! Spud reached down and held up a neatly wrapped bundle with Armour's Ham printed in large bright letters.

"How much did that ham cost you, sonny?" Once again the man was master of the situation.

"A quarter," Spud's voice was low.

"Speak right up, sonny. Nobody's gonna hurt you. Now tell these people what you did to get that ham."

"Just threw three balls in the barrels."

"Easy?"

"Nothing to it," the man's stooge was warming up to his lines.

"Could you do that again? You wouldn't have to pay anything. It's just to show these fine people how easy it is."

"Sure." Spud jumped down, grabbed the three balls, stepped back and measured the distance. The tip of his red-flannel tongue stuck out at the right corner of his mouth. He hadn't lost his cap, but the bill was turned to the back.

It was as easy as coaxing a cat to lap fresh cream. Spud sent the three balls into the barrels and there they stayed until the man reached in and lifted them out.

Spud looked to the crowd for approval.

"See," the man shouted as he shrugged his shoulders in contempt for the failures of the older men. "Nothing to it. I wouldn't let a kid show me up. Who'll try again? Three balls for a quarter, ladies and gentlemen." A carnival barker never forgets his objective.

"Gimme three of them goddam balls. 'Scuse me, ladies," Charlie apologized.

The man pocketed the twenty-five cents and stepped aside. But Charlie did not throw the balls. Rather, he became the interrogator.

"Little Brack," he called Spud by his other nickname. "Can you do that every time?"

"I bleeve so." Spud nodded his head, and his eyes were bright in anticipation.

"Then, here," Charlie shoved the balls into Spud's hands.

"You can't do that," the man spoke sharply. "You bought the balls. You've got to throw them yourself."

"Shut up," Charlie snarled. "Go ahead, Little Brack." Now he mocked the barker. "Nobody's gonna hurt you, sonny. Go ahead; show these people how easy it is."

"It ain't fair," the man yelled. "You can't do that. This is my game and I'll run it as I damn please."

"Apologize to these ladies, mister," Charlie demanded. Then in dead earnest, he continued, "This is a free country, ain't it?"

"Hell, yes," shouted John Rapuzzi who was feeling good from a couple of beers at Knight's saloon.

"Well, if this is a free country, I can give my property away if I want to. Ain't no law to say I can't. Get me?" Charlie looked at the man and flexed his bulging right arm. The argument had attracted more people.

"Okeh, Little Brack, the balls are yours. If you win a ham, I'll give you fifty cents for it. See. Then you can throw and win some more hams to take home to your family. Fair?"

"Sure." Spud was agreeable to everything.

That was the beginning of the end. Spud couldn't miss for hitting.

"Look at Little Brack put that English on them balls."

"Spud sure got the Indian sign on this game."

Everybody was holding out a quarter to him at once. He was grinning benevolently as a gracious Greek god from the heights of Olympus. Finally, the entire rack was empty. The townspeople still stood around. Many of them grinned smugly as they showed the ham or side of bacon tucked under their arms. Spud had not done bad for himself, either.

"Put out some more," the crowd taunted. "Come on, we wanna play."

The man had swelled up like a puff adder. Why didn't Cecil hurry back? Then I saw him pushing through the crowd. Above him towered Dad. He was smiling, and suddenly the world was belted with a rainbow again.

"Look, Uncle Brack," Charlie shouted, "you'll have enough meat to last you 'til hog-killing time again."

"Chip off the old block," Dad laughed proudly, as he walked over to where Spud stood knee-deep in smoked meat.

Who said country folks were dumb? They stood there, Irish, German, Italian, immigrant Polish, Scotch, Welsh, and sundry good American mixtures, around a long-toothed little black boy who wore his cap hind parts before.

The man was furious. He snapped off the lights and stalked away through the crowd. We gathered up the hams and bacon and started home.

Dad was proud of Spud but was still smarting from his shooting gallery experience.

"Ought to come back here tomorrow night and bring my

Winchester," he mumbled. "Bet I'd knock some of them ducks off that rack."

"Oh, I wouldn't bother, Braxton. Everybody knows these games aren't square," Mother comforted.

We were attracted by a terrific pounding. Turning around, we saw a hurriedly made sign being nailed over the now lighted ham and bacon concession. Cecil and I ran back to read it.

"It says, 'Children under sixteen cannot play,'" I reported breathlessly.

We laughed heartily. Dad rubbed the top of Spud's head affectionately.

"Chip off the old block," he murmured, more to himself than to Mother and us children who walked beside him.

12. echoes of Algiers

If you had asked 100 people in Du Quoin the nature of Big Chick's illness, 99 would have told you that he was stricken with brain fever. The hundredth would have leaned over and whispered what at least 50 per cent of the others believed, "Chile, Big Chick's been conjured."

Big Chick's name had been mentioned frequently as checkweighman at Davis' mines. The union election was coming up and those in the know figured Big Chick already in office. That was before his sister, Cerelia, had found him one morning, staring up at the ceiling, unable to move, unable to speak.

Every morning Dr. Gillis stopped by to see how he was getting along. Every night the brothers of the Sir Knight Lodge sat up with him. The women of the neighborhood passed in and out of the three-room house, helping with the cleaning and washing or taking over a plate of choice food that Big Chick scarcely touched.

The finger of suspicion wavered unsteadily in the direction of Lane Gordon, self-styled conjurer, for Lane boasted openly of the "Jack" he carried that made him "master over every nigger in Perry County." Lane had suggested that his boy Chester should be given the berth. Dad tried to reason with Lane. Chester was too young. The job of checkweighman was a juicy plum passed on to a seasoned miner who had won loyalty and respect after years in the pits. Chester wasn't dry behind the ears yet. Undaunted, Lane had talked to other miners, bragging of Chester's ability to handle the job and making veiled threats to anyone who might oppose him.

What the Negroes whispered to each other, Scotch-Irish Maggie Wheatley said right out loud in front of God and everybody. "Maybe somebody's put a spell on Big Chick. I've heard me mither talk aboot it 'appenin' mony a time in the ole country. Tain't natchal, him a-layin' there day after day—not sayin' a word—not makin' a sound." Maggie had stopped in front of our house by the little maple sapling we had planted the spring before. Mother opened her mouth to speak, but upon second thought said nothing. Aunt Dea indulged in a slow wide grin and looked in Mother's direction. "Guess maybe some folks'll believe what we been sayin'. Bless God if they ain't got it in black and white."

Most of the caucus meetings for union activities were held at our house. This was the last meeting they would hold before the election at the union hall in two weeks. Dad, Charlie Brayfield, Button Cunningham, and Will Crayton were sitting around in the front room waiting for Matt Gustatt, union boss of Little Italy.

Cerelia, Big Chick's sister was nearly out of her mind with worry. Otherwise she never would have had the courage to blurt out her troubles before the other men. She had come looking for Dad. It wasn't until after she had whimpered, "Braxton, folks are saying somebody done fixed Big Chick." Then she looked hesitantly about and mumbled an "Excuse me, y'all."

"I wouldn't put no stock in that mess, Cerelia." Dad was

impatient with this evident holdover from the dark age of slavery with its ignorance and superstition.

"God, no!" Will Crayton exploded. "Ain't a damn thing to it. If niggers knowed anything, whyn't they conjured some o' them plague-gone mean white folks in slavery time——" he stopped in confusion as he glanced in Charlie Brayfield's direction. " 'Cuse me Brayfield. I didn't mean no harm. I forgot you was white——"

"I guess that's about the highest compliment you coulda paid me," Brayfield extended his hand to Crayton. "There was no offense meant and none taken, Will. A man can always speak his mind among friends."

"I know—but I didn't want you to think I'd try to show off on you, jes' cause we're three to one. I wasn't cut out that little. But I been hearin' about ghosts an' hants an' conjurin' ever since I was knee-high to a grasshopper. I got chillblains settin' in the graveyard 'til midnight—trying to see something. Used to go outa my way to make black cats cross my path, an' I ain't seen a thing—not a goddamned thing."

Charlie Brayfield fumbled with the wide gold watch chain that hung across his belly. "Well," he drawled, "I can't say as I've seen anything, but I've heard plenty stories. And I know one of the offices of the good fathers is to exorcise evil spirits. I wouldn't say there was nothing to it—no, I wouldn't go that far——"

Cerelia had stood near the door looking from one face to the other, unconsciously smoothing the bedraggled fur collar on her coat. Dad's comment and Will Crayton's strong words had brought a glimmer of hope, but Charlie Brayfield had admitted that the biggest white church in town recognized the existence of such goings on. Now she stood enmeshed in all the old fears and uncertainties. Her voice was tired and hopeless as she begged Dad's pardon for coming over. She pulled the fascinator over her head and turned to go.

"There's bound to be some improvement, Cerelia. Dr. Gillis said——" Cerelia turned away. "Dr. Gillis," she said wearily. "I guess he's doing all he can, Braxton. He said from the first it would take time, but it's awful," her voice sank to a whisper, "day after day—just layin' there—just——"

Dad had crossed over to Cerelia's side. His broad thick hand patted the slight shoulder hunched beneath the heavy coat. "Big Chick's gonna be all right. He's gotta be. We gotta good job comin' up for him. I'll be over in the mornin'——"

The tall figure of Matt Gustatt stepped aside as Cerelia passed out the door. His arrival swung the conversation away from black magic back to the familiar terms of pit boss, checkweighman, and president of Local No. 98.

Dad was up early the next morning. It always gave me a safe warm feeling to lie in bed beneath the heavy woolen quilts, made from the legs of worn-out trousers, and hear Dad moving about in the hazy dawn. If everything was going along all right, Dad's voice could be heard all over the neighborhood:

> King Jesus is a-listenin'
> All night long,
> All night long,
> To hear some sinner pray.

But if something was troubling him, as it evidently was this morning, Dad's voice was soft and pleading. He had a way of singing his prayers. The words were strung closely together, so close that they were not discernible. It was only when there was a change of thought that he lifted his voice above the indistinct chanting in a "An' O Lord!" that wavered between a dramatic tenor and a sonorous baritone voice. His prayer ended, his chores finished, he would enter the house humming his old favorite:

> Shine on me, shine on me,
> Let the light from the lighthouse
> Shine on me——

Aunt Dea was out early, too. She was down to our house before Dad had finished his breakfast. She pulled a chair back from the table and perched herself on the edge of it.

"Buddy," she began slowly, feeling her way. "Don't you think something oughta be done fo' Big Chick?"

"We doin' all we can. Dr. Gillis says it'll jes take time."

"I know what Dr. Gillis say. I'm over there most evva day when he comes. I ain't talkin' 'bout that kinda doin'."

Dad kept his eyes on his plate but he seemed to eat with less and less relish for the savory homemade sausage and the soft scrambled eggs. He did not answer Aunt Dea, so she continued, "You know folks are sayin' somebody done throwed at Big Chick."

"Dea, let's get this straight." Dad pushed his chair back from the table. "I don't wanna get mixed up in this kinda mess. I don't know nothin' about it. I don't believe in it. We ain't got no business raking through dead ashes. Our people done left that stuff behind."

"You can say what you want. Aunt Tempie Sims knows something. She could unfix Big Chick."

Aunt Tempie—the name had a disturbing connotation. The name was never mentioned in careless conversation. It was usually spoken with awe, the same as you mentioned Moses and the plague of hail or lice. Aunt Tempie worked magic, too. Barren women paid good money for her potent love apples that were to make them conceive and bring forth children. Unrequited lovers purchased love powder to make the cold and indifferent adored melt in their arms. It was even rumored that she could locate missing articles and buried treasure. Grandpa Len knew Tempie when she was a young girl, before she had boiled a black cat alive until the meat dropped from the bones. Then taking the potent bone in her right hand, she had gone to the crossroads at midnight on the full of the moon, it was said, and traded her soul to the devil for this strange power she possessed.

Aunt Dea and Dad had been steadily talking while I was busy clipping together rumors of Aunt Tempie's past. Her voice was sharp and impatient. "I don' cear what you believe. You said the same thing when Job was sick. I tole you Aunt Tempie could cure Job."

"Job had the gallopin' consumption, Dea, an' you know it."

"That's what the doctor said. Sure, but what did he know?" Aunt Dea's voice had lost its harshness. It choked and quivered with emotion. "Sendin' Job south to die by hisself among strangers."

"He wasn't among strangers. He was with Sophia's folks."

"Jes the same—I believe Aunt Tempie coulda cured him if you all hadn't a been above askin' her. Jes like Big Chick. Niggers all talkin'—nobody willin' to move a peg."

"All right—all right—I'll go. For God's sake get outa here an' let me finish my breakfast in peace. I gotta work today."

Two days later Dad asked us if we wanted to go for a ride in the country. It was Sunday and the answer was an enthusiastic yes. Spud, Cecil, and I climbed into the two seated spring wagon. Dad lifted the reins and clucked to Prophet, the raw bony horse someone had pulled half frozen from a freight car up in the yards and had given to him.

We waved to the Sadberry children who stood in front of their house with open mouths and questions in their eyes. At the first corner we turned west. The wagon rumbled over the wooden bridge that spanned the ditch. For a while we rode along beside the race track where harness races were held every summer. We could look over and see the ball diamond and the unpainted grandstand. Now we were passing the home of Frank Wells, who kept a grocery store on the East Side. It was a big gray mansion set well back in the yard. Budding maple and birch trees bordered the driveway. The orchard at the back was a gently waving banner of red and white.

There was very little conversation as we jogged along the rutted country roads. Dad was greatly upset. Again he was humming softly to himself. The tune without pattern rose and fell like an escaped passage from a Gregorian chant.

We left the woods that fringed Reese's creek and were now looking out over the freshly plowed rolling fields. The heavily wooded section, commonly known as Beauchoup Bottoms, stretched before us. The road wove in and out among white oak and hickory trees. Patches of sunlight filtered through the branches and fell on clusters of mandrakes that raised their bright-green umbrella leaves. Dad turned off the main road, and Prophet picked his way over the decaying branches and leaf mould that padded the black earth. Ground squirrels chattered like an unwatched teletype machine, scampered a short distance from the road, then sat back on their haunches, watching our approach through their shiny shoe-button eyes.

"Where in the world are we going?" I whispered to Spud. Dad's humming and the silence of the gloomy woods were depressing. Cecil leaned over, nudged Spud, and pointed to Dad, "Ast 'im."

There was no need for questioning. We had reached a small clearing and Dad was pulling Prophet up before a little log cabin that squatted beneath the branches of a towering oak. Cans of dwarfed geraniums sat in rows on the small front porch which had been tacked on to the house as an afterthought. A witch sat on the porch, slowly rocking, a corncob pipe clenched in her crooked stained teeth. Momentarily we expected to see her mount a broomstick and go sailing over the top of the oak tree.

Dad jumped from the wagon and addressed the old woman, "Aunt Tempie?"

She squinted into the sunlight. "That you Braxton?"

"Ain't nobody else."

"What you want?"

"I come about Big Chick."

"Big Chick?"

"That's right, Aunt Tempie."

"Wha's the madda wid Big Chick?"

"Some folks say you oughta know."

Aunt Tempie pulled the plaid shawl closer about her stooped shoulders. The rocker squeaked as it moved back and forth. She took a couple of deep draws from her pipe, tilted her head back, and slowly blew a thin veil of smoke into the hazy air. Spud, Cecil, and I sat huddled in the wagon, scarcely daring to move. Aunt Tempie kept her eyes on Dad's face. "Ah ast ya, wha's the madda wid Big Chick?"

"Dr. Gillis says it's brain fever—but other folks——" Dad looked toward us, then back to Aunt Tempie.

With a woman's intuition she commanded us to get out of the wagon and shooed us off to the woods with a "mine yore wa'k an' stay away f'om the creek bank. Ole Beauchoup mighty sassy this time o' year."

At another time we might have needed this admonition, but not today. Dad's actions had been too strange, and there was nothing in the woods as exciting as the little shriveled figure in the creaking rocker on the porch. We walked slowly through the woods, guided by the sound of swiftly moving water. The creek was high and its muddy waters were tumbling over its own feet as it raced along to join the great Mississippi. We threw in a few twigs, watching them glide sideways out of sight or being pulled under by the swirling eddies in the middle. We turned and raced back toward the clearing.

"Ah nevva woulda give 'em nothin' eff Ah'da knowed they was chunkin' at Big Chick. Nevva in Gawd's world! Speck Ah bettah get on inta town wid you." She held the bowl of the pipe in her hands and sucked her teeth. "Ah know you wonderin' who done it. That ain't fo' me ta say, but Ah'll tell ya dis much." We stopped short, knowing that any movement might cut off the slow flow of words that squeezed themselves through the clenched teeth. "The one who done it is gonna crawl on his belly an' bark lak a dog—jes lak a dog." She looked up in our direction, a half smile playing about her lips. How long had she known we were there? Dad following her gaze became conscious of our presence.

Aunt Tempie hitched herself to the edge of her chair. It was then we noticed the huge black cat that drowsed at her feet. The animal stretched himself and slowly rose to his feet. The gnarled hand of his mistress stroked the thick fur on the arched back. "Coota, you mind evvathing while Ah'm gone." The cat purred and rubbed against the feeble legs. She hobbled into the house and was soon back with a small bundle under her arm. A faded green cape was thrown over her shawl and a rusty black plumed beaver hat was pulled down over her head.

We scrambled into the back seat of the wagon. Dad waited to assist Aunt Tempie.

"Clam on in, son," she ordered. "Ah'll make hit." Dad obeyed without argument. Aunt Tempie reached into the bushes near the porch, pulled a short-handled broom from among the shrubbery and carefully swept the ground about the steps and in front of the house. She walked backwards, sweeping as she came. Not a track remained on the ground, not even her own. When she reached the wagon she flipped the broom back into its hiding place with a dexterity that surprised us. With a few grunts she hoisted herself into the front seat.

Twilight had settled over the prairie before Prophet turned down Walnut Street.

"Wanna stop for a bite to eat, Aunt Tempie?"

"Ain't got time fo' that, Braxton. Take me to Big Chick's. Ah got a lil' unfinished business to take cear of." Dad stopped the wagon in front of Big Chick's, handed the reins to Spud, and leaped to the ground. Aunt Tempie leaned heavily on Dad as she balanced herself on the footrest. Her wide skirts billowed as Dad swung her to the ground.

"Give Prophet a good bait of hay, and don't forget to lock the barn door," Dad called to Spud as Prophet jogged slowly toward our house.

Before Aunt Tempie turned into the yard she ordered us to "Send Dea on up here."

The brothers of the Sir Knight Lodge had just settled themselves for the night when Dad followed Aunt Tempie into Big Chick's cottage. She stood near the door and surveyed the room. Without addressing anybody in particular she made a simple statement, "Too many fo'ks in this room. Somebody got to clear out."

The Sir Knight brothers looked uneasily at each other, then to Cerelia. Cerelia looked at Aunt Tempie, then nodded uncertainly to the two men. They snatched their hats from the table and sidled out of the room. Dad pulled on his hat and started to follow. Aunt Tempie reached a restraining hand toward Dad as she hobbled over to the bed, "Not you, Braxton."

She looked long and hard at Big Chick. Her eyes traveled the length of the bed, resting finally on the immovable face that lay in bold relief on the white pillow case. Having fixed his features clearly in her mind, she cradled slowly over to a chair near the stove and let herself down heavily into it. Aunt Tempie drew her pipe from her pocket, tamped some shredded tobacco leaves into the bowl with her forefinger, and struck a match across the heavy skirt that covered her thighs. Dad sat in a straight chair that was pushed against the north wall.

Aunt Dea entered. Her cheery greeting shivered and froze in the somber silence. She took the walnut rocker on the other side of the stove, looking from Aunt Tempie to Dad, then over to Cerelia who sat huddled on a leather-covered stool at the foot of Big Chick's bed. All were busy with their thoughts and no one seemed conscious that the bobbin was empty of the thread of conversation.

A little moon-faced nickel clock sat on a small shelf above the table. From time to time Aunt Tempie glanced up at the clock. The hands were moving closer to seven. The old woman shifted uneasily in her chair. Dad was as tense as a shot firer watching a kink in a lighted fuse.

As the minute hand moved to twelve, Aunt Tempie rose from her chair. Bending down, she untied her bundle and took out a purple scarf. This she knotted about her head. Her movements were slow and deliberate. There was something of the authority of a high priestess in her actions. Going to the bed she ripped off the covers and spread them down in the northwest corner of the room.

"Hope me git Big Chick onto this pallet," she grunted.

Cerelia, Dad, and Aunt Dea sprang to her aid. Carefully they stretched the unresisting man on the floor and covered his body with the other half of the covers. This done, her old creaking bones seemed to respond to the urgency of the hour. She hurried back to her bag, rummaged around, and finally drew forth some cloth. Kneeling down on the floor, she centered a round piece of yellow silk in a black linen square. She clung to the foot of the bed to pull herself up. The quick movements had caused her breath to come sharply and as she leaned against the brass railing she fished in her dress pocket and drew forth a vicious-looking hooked-blade knife. She opened the blade and moved to the side of the bed.

"Bring that light ovah here, Braxton." Dad, thankful for something to do, jumped to the table and reached for the oil lamp that made a feeble attempt to light the room.

Slitting the ticking, her gnarled hands groped around in

the feather bed. A shower of downy feathers flew into the air. "Come 'ere Dea, an' hol' this tickin'."

Aunt Dea hurried over and lifted the ticking while Aunt Tempie's hand moved among the feathers. In the light of the oil lamp her shadow moved crazily against the wall. Cerelia looked on, scarcely breathing, her eyes wild in her head. Aunt Tempie pulled her hand from the feather bed. At first look it seemed that a few feathers had stuck to her hand, but as she opened it toward the light and peered into it you saw a wad of feathers stuck together by a reddish-brown substance that looked suspiciously like dried blood. She tossed it contemptuously on the yellow circle. Tied to the springs of the bed were little pouches of toe and finger-nail trimmings. She emptied the contents over the wad of feathers and threw the bags into the fire.

Aunt Tempie eyed the sick man for a few minutes, then turned to Cerelia, asking brusquely, "Where the las' clothes Big Chick had on 'fore he took to his bed?"

Cerelia opened the door to a small closet and brought out a shiny brown checkered suit. Without ceremony Aunt Tempie ripped out the lining of the right sleeve. Swinging to the black alpaca was a tiny red flannel hand, complete to veins and fingernails. She hobbled over to the table, humming softly to herself. She turned the lamp wick up a trifle and with her knife slit the short stitches on the hand. From inside she drew forth the tiny shavings of the dried poisonous root of a mandrake bush and a sprig of Solomon's-seal.

Relief was evident in the watery eyes that scrutinized the contents of the "hand." Aunt Tempie sat down on the cane-bottom chair that stood near the table.

"Thank Gawd," she breathed heavily. "Soon as Ah got heah Ah knowed somebody else was 'sponsible fo' Big

Chick's sickness to the p'int o' death. Somebody been mes-
sin' wid mah work, an' Ah don' lak dat a tall." She turned
to Dad. "Braxton, ef Ah cain't hope a soul Ah wouldn't try
to kill 'im." She threw the roots onto the circle. The wad
of feathers was almost to the edge of the square. Aunt
Tempie nudged it back toward the center with her foot.

"This is White Hoss Johnson's work. Ah often said Ah'd
like to hook horns wid him. Sometime yore own prayer send
you wa'kin' through hell fire. Yes, this is ole White Hoss's
work," she repeated. "Lawd, Ah'd know it anywheres. But
bless Gawd, he mus' be gettin' ole caise dis here is false Solomon's-seal. If it hadn'ta been, Big Chick woulda been long
gone."

She stooped down to tie the square into a little bundle.
The small wad of feathers was almost to the edge again.
Aunt Dea eyed it breathlessly. "Great God," she exclaimed,
"the thing's movin'!" Instinctively she moved closer to Dad.

Aunt Tempie kicked the feathers back into the center of
the square and quickly tied the bundle. "Get somethin' on,
Cerelia. You got a long lonesome journey to make tonight."

Cerelia turned toward the closet, then stopped in confusion. Fear struggled with loyalty. She clasped her hands
to her breast and shook her bowed head. "I can't, Aunt
Tempie. I can't. Please don't ask me to go," she pleaded.

"I'm a man," Dad spoke up. "Let me go Aunt Tempie."

"No. Cerelia gotta do it. She's Big Chick's nearest kin.
Hurry chile. Dea can go wid you but she cain't touch this."
She touched the bundle gingerly. "This is yore cross an' you
gotta tote it." Cerelia was buttoning the collar of her coat.
She had tied the fascinator over her head. Impatiently Aunt
Tempie thrust the bundle into Cerelia's hands. "Throw it
in a big stream of runnin' wada," she ordered. "A big stream,

min' you. An' Ah don't cear what you see or hear, don' you turn that bundle loose!"

The next morning Mama insisted that Cerelia come over for breakfast, and she and Aunt Dea talked of nothing but Aunt Tempie's strange potent powers. Several times Mother had tried to switch the conversation but it always came back to the wizened witch of Beauchoup Bottoms. Finally Mother said bluntly, "Dea, I wish you wouldn't talk about that stuff before the children. I don't want them to get that in their heads."

"It ain't what they'll get in their heads what'll hurt 'em," Aunt Dea blew gently into the coffee cooling in the shallow saucer. "It's what some o' these low-down niggers'll get in their bellies if they ain't careful. Yesterday the railroad company brought a carload of section hands up from Louisiana. Them folks is conjurers from 'way back."

Cerelia was also quick to come to Aunt Tempie's defense. For the first time in six weeks Big Chick had said a few words and had fallen off into a natural sleep.

"Ah nevah will forget what she told Cousin Frankie," Aunt Dea added. "Without beatin' the devil around the stump, Tempie came right out an' tole her to quit sweepin' the dirt outa her house after dark. Sweep it up in a corner, or take it up, but don't sweep it outdoors. You sweepin' Mose away f'om home. Frankie ain't paid Tempie no mind, but Mose put his foot in his hand an' lef' an' ain't nevah come back."

Mother saw that there was no hushing them up so she sighed and said by way of concession, "Well, I'm glad nothing happened to you and Cerelia last night."

Aunt Dea and Cerelia exchanged glances. "Who said

nothin' didn't happen?" Aunt Dea wanted to know. "It's a wonder evva hair on my head ain't white. It ain't a hop, skip, and a jump out to Reese's creek an' we had to walk evva blessed step of the way."

"Yes, Lord," Cerelia echoed, "evva blessed step of the way, with thunder and lightning and horses plunging through the sky. That was bad enough, but as we got nearer to the creek all hell broke loose. We heard the groans and cries of a hundred devils. Even when I stood on the bank and was about to throw the bundle into the creek something swooped down from the trees, whipped across my face, and tried to snatch the bundle outa my hands. I held on for dear life and threw the bundle smack into the middle of Reese's creek. The old river snatched at it an' carried it under before a cat could lick her behind. Then all the noises stopped—sudden-like. We stood on the bank in a great silence and I knowed Big Chick was all right. Then we turned back to the road. The morning star glittered and winked at us all the way home. The old moon laid on her back and laughed fit to kill."

13. I've never seen "Uncle Tom's Cabin"

We were returning from school when we noticed the men with their long handled brushes, buckets of paste, and rolls of paper by Old Man Teague's buggy house at the corner of Main and Hickory streets. We stopped to watch as they expertly matched the wide strips against the side of the long shed.

I might have known it! As sure as winter brought mittens and long underwear and etched delicate ivory cathedrals at the bottom of the window panes—it brought *Uncle Tom's Cabin*. These posters were not so exciting and cheerful as the carnival and circus announcements. They spoke of dark and troubled days.

Woolly-headed Uncle Tom sat holding frail little Eva on his knees. Another panel showed bewhiskered Simon Legree and his long-eared bloodhounds chasing Eliza and her baby across the ice. Topsy in pigtails smiled impishly from one corner of the poster.

I hated Topsy! Every time *Uncle Tom's Cabin* came to town, I lost my identity. I am sure Mrs. Harriet Beecher Stowe didn't intend for this to happen, but things are always happening like that in real life. I am sure she wanted to see each one of the 4,000,000 slaves who lived in her time to be known as Fred Baker, John Wallace, or just plain Ann Brown, instead of hearing them referred to as Amos Bishop's nigger, or Sam Gifford's wench. I am sure her concern reached farther than the immediate group of slaves freed by the Emancipation Proclamation. Descending directly from Elijah Holmes who had assured us on numerous occasions that the blood of African kings flowed in our veins, I believe the kind lady "who started the Civil War" wanted me to be called Ruby Berkley.

From past experiences I knew it would be at least a week after Simon Legree had moved his long-eared bloodhounds on to another town before many white children would call me Ruby. It would be "Hello there, Topsy," which was an open declaration of war. I was never disappointed.

I cannot remember a single time when a foreign-born youngster called me this name. They too knew the ordeal of walking with head high as some child stood securely in his yard and yelled Heine, or Wop, or Kike. Of course when assimilation became complete and they became adept at using the latest slang phrases, some of them became offenders too.

Mother had seen *Uncle Tom's Cabin* many times, and though she never issued a directive that we see it she tried to whet our curiosity by her hearty recommendation of the play.

"It's a great play," she would say with enthusiasm. "It sure did a lot for our people in slavery. Some people say it did more to gain our freedom than any other thing."

Helen was the only convert, if convert she could be called. According to Aunt Dee, Helen was born with a "rovin' mind," and the time or place she was going didn't matter much so long as it was out of the Bottoms. The Sadberrys who lived a couple of houses up the street were going en masse. Helen tagged along, unmindful of the many glances cast in her direction for she had the only dark brown face in the stair-step group of freckle-faced half-breeds. The Sadberrys were from the Indian Territory, and despite their membership in the African Methodist Episcopal Zion Church they were accepted with reservations because they ate turtles and had the rather daring picture of the Damn Family on their living-room wall.

Helen kept up a running fire monologue at the breakfast table the next morning. Not only did she tell us the whole story of the play but she had missed very little of the audience reaction. The death of little Eva had brought the house to tears. The brutality of Legree had shamed the white audience into a cold and unnatural silence. The beating to death of Uncle Tom had made the Negroes mad. As Will Crayton had risen from his seat and hurled, "Plague take your time!" to the man on the stage who stood with whip in hand over the quivering body of Uncle Tom, she had sensed the pulling apart of hate.

We were filing out of the front door on our way to school when Mother paused in the act of shaking the dust cloth and said quietly, "Now Ruby, if anybody calls you out of your name this morning, don't pay any attention to them. Just say to yourself, 'Sticks and stones may break my bones but words can never harm me.' "

Are all mothers psychic? I had not mentioned *Uncle Tom's Cabin.* Helen had been deeply touched, but Helen was easily touched. She attended a funeral one afternoon and came home forever committed to the Eastern Star Lodge because she liked the part of the ceremony where they placed a flower in the casket of the departed sister.

I was silent following Mother's advice, but Cecil spoke for me. "What if they call her Topsy, Mama?"

"She should just allow it to their ignorance." Mother set her mouth in a hard straight line and applied the dust cloth with vigor to a surface already polished.

"I get tired of allowing it to their ignorance," I muttered as we reached the sidewalk. "Me too," Spud nodded his head in agreement.

"Maybe they won't today." Cecil was born with an abiding faith in humanity and he never outgrew it.

"They never do when they're in the street. They stay in their yards and call names or throw rocks 'cause they know you can't go in after 'em. But this year I'll get everyone of 'em if it takes me till *Uncle Tom's Cabin* comes to town again," I vowed.

"An' I'll help ya," Spud backed me up.

Cecil's admonition, "You know what Mama said," came too late. Already we were crossing our hearts. Then we shook hands and spat over our right thumbs. The oath was threefold and as potent as though we had signed it in blood.

The trip to school was without incident. Coming home it happened. Spud and I had just joined Katherine Warren who usually waited for us by the Catholic church. Katherine was of Scotch-Irish extraction and lived in the block above us. She was Big Head's baby sister. She came to our house every day. Sometimes we would go to her home but her sisters and brothers were much older than she and her house had grown tired of playing with children. While her father offered some opposition to her frequent visits to our home, Mrs. Warren welcomed and encouraged the association. Loving both of them, Katherine, like Dr. Gillis, reasoned that one skin color might simplify things.

One day she announced that she was going to wash us for dinner. She filled a large pan with water, secured soap and towels from Mother, and washed our hands and faces thoroughly. Spud was several shades darker than I was and when Cecil referred to his own color he would tell you that it was "fast black" and was never known to run. Days later Mrs. Warren gave Mother the whole story behind Katherine's zealous work. Katherine was trying to wash us white!

"Mama," she confided in Mrs. Warren when she finally went home that afternoon, "I can get Ruby pretty clean, but I can't do a thing with Spud or Cecil."

Jackie Rivers lived on the corner of Walnut and South streets. He was eating a slice of homemade bread covered with berry jam. Smudges of jam smeared his face. His auburn hair hung in ringlets and tiny wisps of straw were caught in some of the curls. We liked Jackie. He was smaller than we were but he was a sweet kid.

"Hi Spud. Hello Katherine. Hello Ruby," he greeted us.

As we answered Jackie, his cousin Bristol who lived across the alley came out on the porch and whispered something in his ear. In the same friendly fashion Jackie continued, "Bristol said your name ain't Ruby—it's Topsy."

"It's not either," I informed Jackie.

"He said it is so, too," Jackie insisted. Spud and I looked at each other.

"For shame, Jackie," Katherine chided. "You're a pretty little fellow to go around calling people out of their names."

"You're liable to get hurt," Spud threatened.

"Ain't nobody gonna hurt my little cousin," Bristol swaggered.

"We don't go around beating up babies, but you just step out of that yard and I'll beat the pie outa ya."

Bristol accepted the challenge with, "You and who else?"

Spud's face was screwed into a contemptuous frown. "If I couldn't beat you with one hand tied behind me, you can kick me all the way home."

"Oh yeah?"

"Oh yeah!" Spud had laid aside his mackinaw and was pushing up the sleeves of his woollen sweater. "Come on out. I dare you," he invited.

"We double dare you," I backed up the challenge.

"You shut up, Topsy," Bristol sneered.

Katherine put her arms protectingly about my rigid shoulders. Inwardly I responded to this gesture of friendship but my face held its look of defiance. "Your mama should teach you some manners," Katherine spoke up again. "You're just poor trash—real poor trash!"

"If you're so brave, come on out of your aunt's yard. I dare you to step outside this fence." Spud picked up a small twig and drew a line in front of the gate. "I dare you to come out. Take that dare you'll steal a sheep an' eat his hair."

"If you take that dare, you'll steal a penny off a dead man's eye," I ended. A fellow who wouldn't fight on that dare was a coward. Although we had never seen the practice we had heard that before the days of undertakers, friends would bathe the dead and place a penny on each eye lid to keep it closed.

Katherine picked Spud's mackinaw off the ground and gave it to him. Without so much as another look at Bristol she pulled us along, saying loudly enough for him to hear, "Let's go. Mama always told me if you fool with trash it would fly in your eyes."

Two weeks later we caught Bristol near Geiger's Bakery Shop. He was sucking on a strawberry jawbreaker. We walked up quietly and before he knew it Spud had a firm grip on his collar. "We got you an' ya bette' not call fo' he'p."

Bristol's eyes glowed with the warm light of friendship as he extended a small sack of vari-colored candies. "Want a jawbreaker, Spud?"

We hadn't expected this line of approach. Spud couldn't resist. He reached in and pulled out a large yellow jawbreaker.

"Give Ruby one." Bristol was being generous.

"I like licorice ones."

"Then give her all the licorice ones. I never did like 'em."

We were being bribed and this couldn't happen. We had sworn an oath and we might drop dead any minute if we didn't live up to it. "Remember," I cautioned Spud.

"Aw Ruby," Spud reasoned, "you got four licorice jawbreakers. What more do you want?"

"Nothing—I mean—that is—it ain't that. It's just that we swore. Bristol will understand."

Spud reluctantly held out his jawbreaker to Bristol. "Ruby's right. You see we made a vow that morning that the first kid who called Ruby a name, we'd get 'em. You made Jackie call her a name."

"I didn't mean to make her mad. I didn't mean no real harm, honest." Bristol was anxious to remain on friendly terms.

"You had no business to do that, Bristol, 'cause we crossed our hearts," Spud was dead serious. "You know what that means." I was still holding on to my jawbreakers. "We gotta beat you up. If we don't we'll both drop dead."

Bristol was impressed. He moistened his lips with the tip

146

of his tongue and pulled the motley bill of his cap farther over his forehead.

"Then we spit like this, over our right thumbs." I demonstrated right on the sidewalk in front of Geiger's Bakery window that held pans of sugar cookies and nut bars.

"Golly!" Bristol was as scared as we were. Finally his eyes opened wide. He pushed the bill of his cap back and smiled. He ignored the four licorice jawbreakers I held out to him halfheartedly. "Say, Spud, you didn't say how hard you had to hit a fellow?" We looked at each other and shook our heads vigorously. "Then you and Ruby pop me one, just like you do when a fellow has a birthday. You can hit me as many times as you like, then we can get a dozen sugar cookies. My old man was drunk last night and he gave me a quarter for pullin' off his shoes."

Spud and I swarmed all over Bristol, hitting him playfully about the shoulders. Then we went inside, looked in all the cases, decided on first one thing and then another. It's no fun to ask for what you want right off. We came out of the bakery sucking our jawbreakers and clutching a bag of sugar cookies.

Bristol assured us that he would say a prayer to the Virgin for us. We thanked him but thought such a matter of grave importance should be carried directly to the Head Man himself. We didn't know how God felt about our transaction with Bristol; so we prayed an extra long prayer that night. The next day neither of us dropped dead. For two or three days we were apprehensive, but by the end of the week we figured everything was all right. Evidently God didn't care either.

14. *the stranger within our gates*

Railroad tracks are strange and mysterious things, yet like most commonplace miracles they were taken for granted in Du Quoin. For thousands of miles they lay riveted to wooden ties. If you stood on the tracks near our house and faced south, the tracks seemed to meet down near White Ash mines. But Dad said they didn't. They ran on and on, crossing the muddy Mississippi at Cairo, racing over the heart of Kentucky, sweeping through Tennessee and the Delta, climbing the sloping red clay hills of Alabama, playing tag in and out the bayous of Louisiana until they reached the Gulf.

There was a musical rhythm as the wheels of the cars turned on the tracks. You knew from the sound of the puffing engine whether it had settled itself for a long hard haul, or whether it was deadheading back to the South with a string of empties tacked onto its tail.

There was magic in the names on the box cars: Great Northern, New York Central, Atchison, Topeka, and Santa Fe, Baltimore and Ohio, and the Southern Pacific. Somehow, from somewhere, a master dispatcher had drawn them together and sent them clanking over the Illinois Central roadbed.

It was not until the spring of 1915 that we noticed a strange cargo going north. Black workers from the plantations, artisans from southern cities were flooding the stock-yards of East St. Louis and Chicago.

The lusty adolescent voice of the automobile industry was calling them to Detroit. Men in faded blue overalls and second-hand coats, in tightly fitting cheap suits, hung out of the windows of the dull-colored coaches. Children upon the small laps of ample-bosomed women fretted and slept fitfully as the trains took them farther and farther away from their familiar Southland.

We were near the tracks one day when one of the trains stopped.

"Dis heah is what town?" an elderly man smiled at us.

"Du Quoin!" Spud yelled above the noise of escaping steam.

"Du—what?"

"Du Quoin! Du Quoin!" I repeated.

"Where you goin'?" Spud asked.

"Way up north. To Deestroit," the old man answered proudly.

"Speck we gonna get all freeze up." The woman sitting beside him voiced a fear that had ridden with her from the sunlit doorway of her unpainted cabin.

The engine gave a jerk. The clanking of each coupling traveled the entire length of the train as it moved on toward the insatiable maws of the northern industrial cities.

The miners' coaches had to back up and wait while Charlie Ming switched onto a siding some cars that housed a new group of section hands from Louisiana. These were the first real aliens we had ever seen. I say the "first real aliens" because these men, though bound to us by ties of color, were much more foreign than the immigrant Irish, Polish, German, and Italian workers who came to Du Quoin directly from Ellis Island. We were used to their language, the tight-fitting homespun coats, the long ruffled dresses. They ate our kind of food—steak and chops and potatoes with onions fried in heavy iron skillets. More than that, all the men were miners and were bound together by the common dangers they shared each day in the pits.

The men who had come north from Louisiana did not want to work in the mines. There was a softness about them, as though they had not been toughened by the sun, wind, and rain but had spent most of their time in dimly lighted drawing rooms of a Dumas novel. They were unusually good-looking with a polish that was despised by our men but secretly adored by the women. They were not railroad men but had simply used the free transportation offered by the railroad companies to come north. Most of them soon quit the railroad and found jobs in tailor shops, the St. Nicholas hotel, in Theobald's bakery, and at Will Hayes Bottling Company. But every strange thing is ugly.

Among the newcomers, the youngest was Pierre Le Blanc. Tall and slim, there was the dash of the courtier about him. His well-modulated voice was heavy with a French accent. As we came face to face with him on the streets, reluctantly obeying the ultimatum of the older folks, we met the eager friendliness in his eyes with averted glances and closed lips.

He usually walked alone. Like the pricking of an ever-present conscience, we met him in many places. His French-Negroid features were chiseled of mellowed ivory, his curly dark brown hair invited the play of feminine fingers.

Sometimes he stood on the corner with a group of older Creoles. Their conversation was animated. Their long, tapering fingers and the shrug of their shoulders added as much to their talk as the words they spoke. Le Blanc was the most romantic figure in our town and our curiosity was whetted because of the taboo our elders had created about him and his kind.

"I asked Adam Devereau if he come from Algiers," Uncle George, the town constable, was talking to Dad one evening as they sat on our front steps.

"Ain't that in some foreign country?" Dad wasn't too sure of his geography.

"Naw." Uncle George shook a loose front tooth with his right thumb. "Reckon I oughta pull that tooth, but when I do I won't have nare chair in my parlor. As I was saying, Algiers ain't no foreign country. It's a town in Louisiana where the ole king conjurers live."

"Naw."

"Yeah. All of 'em are smart in black magic. Thas why I told you to tell Helen to stay away from them men. All of 'em carry a pocket full of John the Conqueror root and plenty of love powder. Can't no woman stand up against 'em."

"I never did bleeve too much in this sprinklin' business," Dad said lightly, but added cautiously, "just the same you can't be too careful."

"I'll say you can't." Aunt Belle had come over from her house across the street. "Look what happened to Cicero and Fannie when they took Francois to board."

"You can't be too hard on Fannie, Belle," Uncle George reasoned. "For the last ten years she ain't had nothing but beatin's and cussin' from Cicero. He wouldn't work and he drank up all she made."

"Don't make no difference. She'd stuck with him through

thick an' thin until that Francois went to live with 'em. Then another thing George Smith, they don't even eat like God-fearing Americans. Ever pass by when they was cooking? I ain't never smelled such cooking."

"It's good, Aunt Belle," I chimed in. "I ate some gumbo over to Miss Farquhar's. It had chicken and shrimps and it was kinda ropey like it had lotsa okra in it, but Miss Farquhar said it was the felee that made it green and stringy."

"Great Gawd A'mighty, Ruby," Aunt Belle was horrified. "You gonna come up dead, eatin' after all these strange niggers."

"Unca Brack! Unca Brack!" Cornie Clary came running down the street. "Unca Brack, ole Snake Doctor done shot Pierre Le Blanc!"

"Shot him?" Dad and Uncle George were on their feet and halfway to the sidewalk.

"He's laying down there on the corner by Liza Roach's house. He ain't breathin'. Speck he's dead."

"You kids stay in this yard." Already we had started to follow.

Because Snake Doctor was a familiar figure on the streets of Du Quoin we tried to justify his actions though he had never been a visitor at any of our homes. The men knew him because he worked on the railroad and sometimes shot a poor game of pool at John Simmon's pool hall. The women and children knew him because he was a bullet-headed, lanky, ungainly fellow who came into town at two-week intervals, and according to rumor, willingly gave up his entire check to olive-complexioned Mabel Carter for a few hours of questionable pleasure.

Dad and Uncle George came back a few hours later. They were silent. Mother's gentle prodding and Aunt Belle's insistence failed to bring forth the desired information. Several other neighbors sauntered over.

"My Gawd, Braxton, it can't be no secret," Aunt Belle was exasperated. "The man is dead. Laid up there on Liza Roach's corner for two hours, didn't he? Everybody knows that Snake Doctor shot him. Says he did it in self defense. Says Le Blanc pulled a knife on him."

From Cora Simpson we knew that Dad and Uncle George had been with Police Chief Charlie Layman when Snake Doctor gave himself up. They had been there when the doctor had pronounced Le Blanc dead, and at the coroner's request had helped Charlie Weinberg place the body in the long basket and had stood there after he had driven away to his undertaking parlor.

Dad's lips moved but the words were unintelligible to us.

"What you mumbling like an ole woman to yourself for?" Aunt Belle wanted to know.

"He was such a clean-looking boy." Dad was still talking to himself.

"He couldn'ta been too clean. He was living at Mabel Carter's house," Aunt Belle reminded Dad.

"Did you offer him a room? Did I try to get him a place with decent people?"

"No need to reproach yourself, Braxton." Mother tried to justify Du Quoin's indifference to Le Blanc and his kind. "If he'd a been the right sort he never would have gone to that kind of house. Water seeks its own level."

"His room was fulla books. Mabel said he jes set an' read most of the time. Some of 'em was in a foreign language, said she thought they was in French. Then she said he would go walking at night. Sometimes he'd walk as far as St. John's Grove. Said he missed the parties and his friends back home."

"That still don't do away with the fact that he tried to knife Snake Doctor. Them southern niggers always using a knife." Almenzona Davis, just two winters removed from the bowels of Georgia, shifted her snuff brush and drew a small can of Garrett from her apron pocket.

"They ain't found no knife," Dad said quietly. "Liza Roach is as truthful a white woman as ever set foot in Du Quoin. She was settin' on her front porch an' seen everything. She said Le Blanc didn't reach for nothing. Snake Doctor spoke to him—then pulled his gun. Looks like he done stole that pore boy's life."

The night air was sweet with a honeysuckle vine that climbed a rickety trellis.

"I guess they'll be shipping his body back home after the inquest. Wonder if his mother is still living?" Mother asked more to fill in the awkward silence than for information.

"Yes, his mother is still living."

There was no more talk that night. Deep in thought, the neighbors drifted away. Some of them did not even say good night.

Next morning Mother answered a knock at our front door.

"Oh, it's you, Miss Carter. Won't you come in?" Mabel entered the living room and seated herself in the cane-bottomed rocker near the door. There was no make-up on her olive-tinted face.

"Mrs. Berkley—I hope you forgive me for coming to your house." She drew a yellow envelope from her handbag and gave it to Mother. "Read it and tell me what to do."

"So she's coming here," Mother gave the folded paper back to Mabel.

"Yes. And she wants to meet all his friends at the wake."

"What friends?"

"She must not know, Mrs. Berkley. We can't let her know that he had no friends."

"She can't help but know once she is here."

"I suppose it's too much to ask—but I was hoping the people could be different with her. She has enough to bear. I'm not asking it for myself, but," Mabel bit her lower lip in desperation, "I was hoping that you and Mr. Berkley could help me work out something. She's only going to be here a day and a night."

"Did he say what his mother does? What is she like?"

Again Mabel's hand fished in her bag. She gave Mother a small picture set in a gold frame.

"She's beautiful," Mother gazed without envy upon the clear hazel eyes, the dark hair waved back from the high, unwrinkled forehead.

"She teaches school in New Orleans. Pierre told me. He worshipped her. She didn't want him to come north, but he thought he could make enough money to finish college. He only had another year to go."

"And she wants the wake at your house." Mother emphasized no word. She was just trying to get the details straight in her own mind.

"Yes, Mrs. Berkley—but you see she doesn't know. She just knows that Pierre lived at my house. If anybody can help me, I know you and Mr. Berkley will."

Mabel Carter's house was a neat white frame house trimmed with yellow shutters. Set well back of a white picket fence on Chestnut Street, it faced the tracks from whence came much of her trade. Even we kids knew that she was the highest paid colored prostitute in town. Four girls stayed with her. Leona, a round-faced, statuesque, dark girl was frequently referred to as Black Beauty. Faye was a frail, consumptive, moon-eyed creature with a low, husky voice. Sadie, who was a dead ringer for Theda Bara, could have stepped across the color-line any day in the week. Ruth, who just stopped short of being a midget, was brown, bowlegged and a little on the chunky side. They were not the cheap, common Oak Street variety, who were not above soliciting trade on the streets. Mabel's actions on the streets were always above reproach. She wore expensive clothes, but they were always in good taste. A large solitaire on her ring finger and sheer silk stockings on her shapely legs were the only insignia of her age-old profession.

The night of the wake saw a crowd strange to the walls of Mabel's rooms. Mrs. Le Blanc moved about at Mabel's elbow, grief-stricken, but quiet and gracious. Professor and Mrs. Mosby, the entire teaching staff of Lincoln School, the Methodist minister, Rev. S. D. Davis and his wife, Dr. Zephaniah Green, the town's only Negro doctor, and all the respectable colored people were there. Mother and Dad had done their job well.

Crepe hung outside the door to show that the house was in mourning. Eli Gregory had stationed himself on the porch to keep out anyone who might be too drunk to recognize the meaning of the wreath and ribbons.

We heard Mother and Aunt Dea tell Cousin Frankie

about it the next morning. She had walked unaccompanied from her house.

"Frankie, it was the saddest thing you ever saw," Aunt Dea began.

"I didn't sleep a wink last night after we came home," Mother admitted. "I just lay there thinking. I kept seeing the body in Mabel's room. A crucifix hung above the small dressing table and the tall candles seemed to convert it into an altar."

"We had no spirit for singing but we sung a few songs," Aunt Dea continued. "Then some of Pierre's friends started to sing."

"It was a Creole lullaby," Mother explained. "It was a shy, plaintive thing, as though a mother were placing her child tenderly in the arms of Jesus. Bernadine Le Blanc clung to Mabel Carter. The whole house was in tears. Rev. Davis fished his handkerchief from the hind pocket of his swallow-tail coat. It was awful."

"But Sophia, do you know that was the first time in my life I knowed that Jesus was in favor of the Republican party," Aunt Dea mused.

"Jesus in favor of the Republican party?" Mother repeated incredibly.

"Why yes. You remember what Rev. Davis said. 'Course I always voted the Republican ticket because Abe Lincoln freed the slaves and Buddy is on the Republican Central Committee. Just goes to show you can't get ahead of the Old Book."

Mother smiled faintly, for even the humor of Aunt Dea reading something foreign into the simple scripture Rev. Davis had quoted could not take away the solemnity of the preceding night.

"What did Rev. Davis say?" Cousin Frankie wanted to know.

"After Pierre's friends had finished their song, Rev. Davis stood up to say a few words. He spoke of Christian charity that included the stranger within our gates. His voice was kindly but his words cut us with a thousand lashes," Mother was carefully trying to recreate the scene for Cousin Frankie.

"Woe unto those by whom offense comes, was the first scripture he quoted. It were better for him that a millstone were about his neck and he were cast into the midst of the sea, than that he should offend one of the least of these. Some people listen to the word of God with a pitchfork and some listen with a rake. Whatever the minister says, the fellow with the pitchfork says, he ain't talking about me, he's talking about brother John, so he pitches God's truth over on somebody else. But the fellow with the rake pulls everything to him. He says, whatever it is, it's for me. I want all of you to throw away your pitchforks and get your rakes for I'm talking to all of you and I'm putting myself in for good measure. For the first time in my life I understand what the Christ meant when he said, 'I say unto you that the publicans and the harlots go into the Kingdom of Heaven before you!'

"No one noticed Mrs. Le Blanc as she slipped quietly from the room. We only saw her returning with an armful of books. She walked over to Rev. Davis and held out a letter to him. We were shocked by her strange words."

"I have learned to love you all through Pierre's eyes. Even before I came I knew the church and the parochial school where the tall father walks up and down, up and down in the cool of the twilight. I knew of the hay rides on moonlit nights when the young people built a fire by Big Muddy

Creek, then rode home waking the farmers and the towns-people with their carefree singing. It is there." She pointed to the letter in Reverend Davis' hand. "Please read—just the postscript—it is enough."

"You spoke of discerning a trace of loneliness in my last letter Mama," Rev. Davis read. "Maybe the loneliness comes from your own mother heart for her youngest born who is so far away from home. You would love these people, ma mère. The African Methodist Episcopal Zion Church has a roller skating rink and many young people go there every night. The Baptist Church, named for the good St. Paul, has a lighted court where you can play croquet in the evening. This is a nice little town, ma mère, and I know if you ever come here you will love it as I do."

"Chile, you coulda heard a pin drop. My Lord." Aunt Dea groaned with the agony of remembering. "That boy sho heaped coals of fire on our heads."

"And gracious Bernadine Le Blanc was adding fuel to the flames," Mother added. "We should have been trying to comfort her, but instinctively she sensed that she should comfort us."

"Maybe you do not read Pierre's native language in which many of his books are written," she said, "but I want to leave his best loved possessions among his kind friends." She passed among the people, giving each one a volume from Pierre's bookshelves. Mabel, Leona, and Sadie followed with other books by Dumas, Balzac, De Maupassant, Verne, Zola, authors strange to most of the people of our little town.

The fast Daylight Express puffed to a stop. Charlie Weinberg, Reese Springs, Button Cunningham, Dad, and Uncle Robert slid the long box into the baggage car. Mrs. Le

Blanc, loaded down with fried chicken, milk-chocolate cake, baskets of fruit, and boxes of candy, found a seat in the day coach. Soon the engineer blew his whistle. The engine gave a jerk and the clanking of each coupling traveled the length of the train. It was soon out of sight. We stood on the tracks. They seemed to meet down near White Ash mines. But Dad said they didn't.

The fast passenger train raced toward the Southland. It crossed the muddy Mississippi at Cairo, raced over the heart of Kentucky, swept on through Tennessee and the Delta, climbed the sloping red clay hills of Alabama, played tag in and out of the bayous of Louisiana until it reached the Gulf with a sorrowing mother and the body of her son who was now beyond the bigotry and indifference of a small town.

15. *we attend a baptizing*

Baptizings were always held at Blakesley's old mill pond on North Walnut Street. A small grove of trees gave the place the air of a private park and it was always used by young lovers who wanted a bit of solitude and beauty as a backdrop for romance.

The west and north sides of the pond were fenced to give protection to passers-by on the street and to the small children who played in Ada McKnight's yard. The south bank sloped sharply down to the water. This Sunday afternoon the south bank was crowded with Baptists, Methodists, Old Man Crayton, the lone Negro convert to Catholicism, the sinners, Jim Blake, who proudly called himself an infidel, and a few young rowdies who came to see how the wet robes hugged the women converts when they came up out of the water.

This was Mt. Olive's big day and Reverend Stuart was making the most of it. He lifted his right hand for silence and all conversation ceased. Beyond the west fence a few white people watched from a respectful distance.

> I'm going down to the big baptizin',
> I'm going down to the big baptizin'
> Some of these days, Hallelujah,
> I'm going down to the big baptizin'
> I'm going down to the big baptizin'
> Some of these days.

> I'm gonna shake hands with my Jesus,
> I'm gonna shake hands with my Jesus,
> Some of these days, Hallelujah,
> I'm gonna shake hands with my Jesus,
> I'm gonna shake hands with my Jesus,
> Some of these days.

> I'm gonna tell Him how you treat me,
> Oh yes, I'm gonna tell Him how you treat me
> Some of these days, Hallelujah——

"Yes!" Aunt Mandy Stigall, overcome with emotion, shouted above the singing. "You know, sweet Jesus!"

The eyes of the white people left the large group of singing Negroes and found interest in the colorful leaves of the maple trees.

> I'm gonna tell Him how you treat me,
> I'm gonna tell Him how you treat me
> Some of these days.

By this time Elder Ross was assisting Reverend Stuart as he waded into the water. Deacon Tinsley had walked before them sounding the depth of the water with a long staff-like pole. When Moses stretched forth his hand and led the children of Israel across Jordan he could not have done it with more solemnity than these three who were now executing the Lord's business. Deacon Tinsley stopped, planted his staff in the soft mud of the pond. Elder Ross assisted Reverend Stuart as he turned slowly about to face the congregation.

> I'm going down to the big baptizing,
> Oh yes, I'm going down to the big baptizing
> Some of these days, Hallelujah.

Elder Ross held the hem of Reverend Stuart's robe in the water until the weight of the dampness caused the cloth to sink.

> I'm going down to the big baptizing—
> Some of these days.

"Dear Heavenly Father, it is once more and again, we your humble children have assembled together in accordance with Thy divine order to receive a few more of Thy sheep into the fold." Reverend Stuart's prayer sped on its way to the battlements of glory buoyed by a chorus of "Yes, Lord" and "Amen, Jesus."

"Lord, we believe You knowed what You was talking about when You said to baptize the believers. We know You meant what You said when You sent Your disciples forth to baptize in Your name. Lord, we know if You hadda meant for us to take a pitcher of water and sprinkle it over the converts' heads, You woulda told us so. If that was all You was gonna do You wouldna wasted Your precious time walking all the way out to the River Jordan to do it."

The Methodists in the crowd were getting restless. It was unfair to attack an opponent who could not defend himself. We knew however that Reverend Davis' sermon the next Sunday would include the scripture, "I will sprinkle your head with clear water——"

Reverend Stuart, giving, as he was wont to say, no space for the devil, marched on boldly to the throne of grace.

"Hover over this place this afternoon, Gracious God. May everything said and done here be done to the honor and glory of Thy name. These blessings we ask in the name of Thy dear son, Christ Jesus. Amen."

The converts stood surrounded and partially obscured by the deaconesses in their billowing white dresses. At the end of the prayer they were led nearer to the water. The preacher reached forth his arms and Deacon Tinsley accompanied the first convert into the water. Someone on the bank raised a song:

> Here's another one coming to be baptized,
> To be baptized, be baptized;
> Here's another one coming to be baptized
> To view the dyin' lamb.

The convert was now safely in the hands of Elder Ross and Reverend Stuart. They whispered something to him. He nodded his head with enthusiasm. Raising his right hand above the bowed head, Reverend Stuart intoned:

"According to the confession of your faith and in fulfillment to the commandment of Jesus Christ, I baptize you in the name of the Father, and of the Son, and of the Holy Ghost. Amen."

The convert was completely immersed. A split second later he was raised from the watery grave to walk in the newness of life. A mother on the bank screamed and the convert leaped in the water, shouting and praising God. He needed no assistance but waded boldly ashore to be clasped in his mother's arms. Unmindful of his wet clothes, she hugged and kissed him. Finally the young man was led to a home nearby where he could change into dry clothing.

Several other candidates followed in rapid succession. It was getting to be rather routine when Sister Smith started leading Ella Jenkins down to the water. We first heard the feeble but insistent protests above the singing.

> Here's another one coming to be baptized,
> Be baptized, be baptized——

"Please don' put me in that water, please don' put me in that water——" The high-pitched childish voice ran like a discord through the swinging chorus. The deaconess half pulled, half coaxed the unwilling candidate along.

Deacon Tinsley had sized up the situation. He took the girl from the deaconess and whispered a few words to her. Ella's voice dropped to a whimper and she was led into the water. Her lips were still moving, not in prayer to God but in entreaty to the people who were compelling her to go through the ceremony.

The minister whispered to Elder Ross who kept up the singing as Reverend Stuart said the words over the candidate. Now the trembling figure was buried beneath the water. As the slender body rose above the surface of the water, a piercing scream rent the air. It was not the joyous sound of a rejoicing believer. It was a cry of terror.

Eluding the slippery tired hands of Reverend Stuart and Elder Ross, Ella Jenkins scrambled out of the water. Two deaconesses waited on the bank with a warm blanket to put around the screaming girl.

Ella paused for a moment, and as the women advanced she recognized them as the ones who had led her into the water against her will. Side-stepping their waiting arms, she cut a path through the crowd and raced for home.

The Baptists looked at the fleeing girl and sadly shook their heads.

"Poor child, the devil must own her lock, stock, and barrel," Old Lady Criddon shook her head and shifted her snuff brush to the other side of her mouth.

"Poor little thing. She never was real bright," Charity Boyd murmured. Some of the other Methodists doubled over with laughter.

Dad was gripping my hand tight. He was neither chagrined nor amused. He was mad.

"They shouldn'ta done it," he muttered. "Jesus was kind to little children. He didn't go around scaring 'em to death."

16. *strike!*

In many parts of the country the first robin is called the harbinger of spring. Du Quoin had dozens of signs. Apple trees with blooms of white tinged with pink, cherry trees in festive colors of white and red suspended brilliant patches of beauty above the mud-filled ruts called roads. Lace curtains rid of the black coal dust of a long winter season were white and even on Frances Hunter's curtain stretchers.

Deep purple hyacinths, golden jonquils, and vari-colored tulips lined the cement walk that led to Amelia Young's front steps. A tall bush that had stood denuded in the biting winter wind now flaunted virgin white blooms shaped like assorted sizes of popcorn balls. Shoots of portulaca were uncurling their tiny fists in the wire baskets that hung on Kate Seaman's porch.

Every child was thoroughly dosed with sulphur and molasses to purify the blood. Mass discarding of long-legged underwear, that had given the impression of a whole populace afflicted with extreme cases of varicose veins, was now in progress. When these things came to pass, no matter what happened on Ground Hog Day, you were safe in saying spring had come.

But the most positive sign had nothing to do with budding trees, flowers, or blood tonics. The first casual mentioning of an impending strike that would rise to crescendo heights before the walkout or lockout began, was one of the surest signs.

Yancey Boyd surveyed the groceries and meat piled before him on the counter of Forester's company store.

"We'll eat for a while anyway," he smiled at young Matt Gustatt, who was rechecking and listing the purchases in the company book.

"You sure will, Mr. Boyd." Matt kept writing while he made conversation. "Fellow has to buy pretty careful now. If the men strike, some of them will have to be cut off."

"Did Eddley Thornton say that?" Boyd wanted to know.

"Oh, no. Just a matter of deduction. You can't tell how long the mines will be shut down. It will be impossible for the store to extend credit to all the men, as much as we'd like to."

Boyd tapped on his protruding stomach that completely hid his belt buckle. "I can afford to miss a few meals."

"I was just looking at that pouch," Arky Knight slapped Boyd on the back playfully. "What's it gonna be, Yancey? Pups? Well, I'll take the speckled one."

"Watch your talk, men." Charlie McCollums never laughed at anything. "There are women in the store. What'll it be for you, Little Brack?"

Many people called both Spud and me "Little Brack." Spud was given the added "little" to distinguish between him and Dad, for both had the same name. They called me Little Brack because, even though I was a girl, most folks said I was born for good luck, being the spitting image of Dad.

"Mother sent this butter back. It's rancid, she said." I shoved a sack with a pound of butter in it upon the counter.

168

"Didn't know you ever bought butter." Charlie McCollums took the butter and sniffed it. "Thought you had a cow."

"We don't usually, but Cherry's dry. She won't come fresh 'til August."

"I'll go back in the refrigerator and find your mother a good pound. We just got some in today. Sophia knows value. Said the other was rancid, did she?"

"She said it was strong enough to walk." I told him Mother's exact words.

For a minute it seemed that a little smile would break through. Then the playful wrinkles about the mouth settled themselves in their customary straight line and Charlie went into the storeroom.

"Matt Gustatt said the miners gonna strike this year, Dad." We were eating brisket stew that had been lightly seasoned with onions and garlic. Whole carrots and small potatoes floated in the thick brown gravy.

"Not again, Braxton," Mother's voice was tinged with irritation.

"Why not?" Dad wanted to know.

"Every year it's the same thing."

"We don't strike every year."

"It seems like it to me. You're either striking for higher wages, or out of sympathy with the miners in Ashley or Kentucky, or something," Mother finished lamely.

"I didn't know you was on the other side of the fence. You don't seem to remember the times the operators locked us out because they couldn't get the price they wanted for their coal. We didn't want to stop work. What do they do? They ups and takes their families to Florida and loll around in the sunshine. We could set on our behinds and starve and freeze for all they cared."

"I know that, too, but——"

"Everything we've got we had to strike to get it. The operators and owners ain't never come up an' handed us anything out of a clear sky. The miner ain't got but one trump card to play. If that don't take the trick, we're through."

Mother sighed wistfully. "I thought maybe this year we could build on another bedroom. Helen and Ruby really need one. They don't have any privacy sleeping in the living room. Looks like we'll never get ahead."

"Women ain't never satisfied." Dad's voice had taken on a lightness the conversation did not warrant. He pushed his chair back from the table. "There's a meeting of the pit committee tonight. I gotta be going."

Dad was looking at Mother strangely. I expected to see him walk around the table and give her a reassuring pat on the shoulder. He stood by his chair for a minute, then pushed it under the table. Going into the bedroom, he was soon back with his brown Stetson and a lightweight gabardine topcoat. When he reached the outside kitchen door, he stopped and looked at Mother.

"Don't you worry none, Sophia. We'll come out on top. We always manage somehow—at least you do. As long as there's enough for you and the kids, I'm happy. I don't wanna get rich an' have indigestion."

Mother didn't answer, but her face lost its worried look. Again she was the peaceful, poised woman whose quiet strength matched the iron in our dad's character. Somehow in the magical alchemy of thought they were again one. We sensed this and knew we had nothing to fear.

strike!

The walkout was called for the fifth of May. The first few weeks were uneventful. Most of the men spaded or plowed plots for the summer garden. Rickety steps were reinforced. Loose palings were hammered into place. Small fishing parties, immovable as Indian scouts, dotted the lush banks of Big Muddy Creek. The crowds grew larger in front of John Simmon's pool hall. The swinging doors to Lew Smith's saloon were seldom motionless. The town took on a holiday air.

The company stores were not crowded. Housewives, familiar with strikes, their duration and company store credit, were buying the bare necessities. Mother, Aunt Dea, Aunt Belle, and Lettie Clary spent hours bending their backs to find the tiny shoots of lamb's quarter, wild mustard, polk salad, and narrow dock that grew sparsely on the prairies. The tender leaves would be washed thoroughly and cooked with a ham hock or small strips of bacon rind.

Meetings of the operators and the striking miners left sullen groups of workers under the gaslights on the street corners mapping stratagem to end the deadlock. The miners were insisting on the unheard of minimum wage of eight dollars per day and worker's compensation in case of sickness or injury.

"We'd go broke," Ross Deadmann spoke for the operators. "That compensation will breed a lot of lazy men. Everybody's looking for something for nothing."

"A miner don't get something for nothing," Dad challenged him. "Every time a miner goes down the cage he takes his life in his own hands or puts it in the hands of any greenhorn that has been hired. You ain't givin' us nothin', Ross Deadmann. You don't know what a miner's worth. Have you ever crawled around on the bottom like a

171

squint-eyed mole? When I first went in the mines we worked from cain't see to cain't see—twelve hours a day for a dollar an' thirty-five cents. We gonna be playin' catch-up for a long time."

By the last of June, the gardens were coming to the aid of the miners. Lettuce and tender green onions could be shredded and wilted with hot vinegar and bacon grease. Turnip tops could be used for greens. The corn was standing well over a foot high. Kentucky wonders were fastening their tendrils around the slender poles placed for them to climb on. Irish potato plants were squatting like miniature umbrella trees. Melon and squash vines were spreading over the warm brown earth. But even as the miners looked with pride over the little gardens that were to be their shields against hunger, the sky withheld its rain. The hot July sun scorched the earth and turned the patches of green into charred dry wastes.

The operators refused to meet with the union representatives. The vacation was over. Open warfare had been declared. The miners seemed to be on the losing side. No work, no credit, no food, and hungry children were tipping the scales in favor of an early settlement with no gains for the workers.

A bushel basket of apples sat on the pantry floor. There was no connection in our minds between the apples and Henry Tillman, a white neighbor, leaving our yard with a sack of flour, until the evening paper carried an account of burglars raiding Old Man Lipe's apple orchard the night before.

"A man'll beg before he steals, but he'll sure steal before he starves." Aunt Dea seemed to be talking more to herself than anyone else. Without being told, we sensed that we were not to talk about the apples.

Our dinner table took on more and more the aspects of an international peace parley. Jan Borinski and his blonde sister Helga, Polish youngsters from the next block, often came to play and stayed until Mother had set the table. Joe Sorato from Little Italy became an initiate and enthusiast of beans, pot licker, and corn bread. Patrick O'Connell and his brother Barry, second generation sons of Erin, would come over and without any pretext or hesitation, ask for bread and jelly.

"You can't feed the whole town," Aunt Dea told Dad, after several children had been fed and sent home.

"If he isn't feeding the children, he's bulldozing Eddley Thornton into giving their daddies credit at the company store. He's stood good for more than a dozen miners."

"I ain't the only one. Charlie Brayfield and Pete Solomon's gone to bat for some of the men. They'll pay up as soon as they get to work. I ain't worried about losing anything. I couldn't eat if I thought these children was hungry. We wrote to headquarters but we ain't heard a word. I cain't understand it."

"Buddy," Aunt Dea hesitated as though by the mere speaking she would call into consequence the thing she feared, "I've heard some talk. Is there any truth to it? Are the operators going to bring in *scabs?*"

At last it was said and we waited breathlessly for the answer that was slow in coming.

"There's some talk of it."

Aunt Dea's voice was filled with contempt. "Dirty, low-down whelps."

"Some men don't understand."

"They understand they're taking other men's jobs. They're taking bread an' meat out of women and children's mouths. They got what was coming to 'em at Zeigler."

"They won't take our jobs." Dad's voice was calm and even, but a hardness had crept into his last words.

"Who's to stop them?"

"They can be stopped." His answer was simple, but deadly.

In the quiet that followed we were busy reconstructing the other times that scabs had been stopped.

There was the time when the operators were bringing a carload of Italian immigrants straight from Ellis Island to break strike. Armed with only his mother tongue and a borrowed homespun suit, Joe Fantaco had boarded the train above Kankakee and signed up every man in the coach as a member of the union before it reached Du Quoin.

The explosion at Zeigler was never discussed, yet what had happened was common knowledge. The strike had dragged on for months. Then one day as the surly miners looked on, smoke rose from the engine house and coal was being hoisted to the top. One hundred Negroes from Kentucky had been slipped into the mines on the previous evening. The next day another Negro walked boldly up to the office and asked for a job. The operators smiled, thinking that it would only be a short time before all the miners would return with humble pie in their teeth.

Late that afternoon a series of explosions shook the mine. The earth swayed with the reverberations. Below, the timbers wrenched themselves from the roofs of the coal seams and blocked the entries. Tracks were twisted and above the splintering of the wood and the sliding of coal and slate, the curses and groans of wounded and dying men and animals were lost. Rescue crews found the passages completely blocked by tons of debris. After a month of trying to drill through to a clear passage, the operators decided to abandon the mines and seal the entrance. With mixed emotions the townspeople gathered at the mines where services were to be held for the unfortunate men.

The minister spoke with feeling of the brave men who had perished in the untimely explosion. The miners knew that the explosion was not untimely. It was timed to perfection. The lone miner who had walked boldly up to the office and applied for a job was an expert shot firer from upstate. If anyone had been watching they would have seen him climb up the ladder and get into a waiting surrey just a few minutes before the explosion.

We were not fooled the next day by the announcement that a few of the men were going rabbit hunting. The early morning had been spent with oiling and cleaning pumps and Winchesters. Cartridge belts were filled with shells and a generous supply bulged from the wide pockets of the hunting jackets. As we watched Dad, Uncle Robert, Ernest Smith, and Willie Turner go down the street, we saw a group of four or five Polish miners join the bunch. Their backs were to us and we could not tell who they were, but there was no mistaking the massive figure of Henry Diedeffer, the German checkweighman. There was something sinister and frightening, for, as the group went down the street, other figures stepped out to join them.

"Mama, I thought Dad said rabbits were no good in the summer. He's never killed any before this time of year," Cecil questioned.

"This is a different kind of rabbit, I guess." Mother always tried to answer our questions.

"But there ain't but one kind of rabbit 'round here. Ain't nothing but cottontails, is there, Mama?"

Mother evidently didn't hear Cecil, for she did not answer.

"It's not rabbits they're hunting. Rabbits got little babies and worms in 'em in July," Jan Borinski whispered. "They're out to stop the scabs."

"How do you know?" I demanded.

"My old man said so this morning. The scabs are to get off the train at eleven o'clock at Pinkneyville. The operators are gonna walk 'em through St. Johns and on out to the mines."

Mother must have heard Jan's whispered explanation, for she said quietly, "I'm sure your father does not want you to repeat what he told your mother in confidence."

We followed Jan outside where he could give us more details without grown-up censure or interference.

The women formed gossip squads and hung over their front gates. Boys grouped themselves under shade trees and played a listless game of marbles. Girls sat on the front porches and played jacks or dressed dolls. Today the game was not important. Tomorrow Spud and Cecil would come home with their pockets filled with the best aggies in the neighborhood, but today there was only the need of understanding friends close by. Something was going on that we had never experienced before.

Mother made herself busy cleaning the pantry shelves. I cut the newspaper edges into scallops and added patterns of triangular and rectangular shapes. I was glad when Kate Seaman, our German neighbor who lived next door to the north, came over with her basket of stockings to darn. Evidently Aunt Ida, Aunt Belle, and Mrs. Sadberry had seen her coming, for soon the older women had nearly crowded the children from the porch. German, Italian, Polish, and Negro women too sought comfort in each other's company.

There was small talk about Old Man Gant bringing his first scrawny melons into town and asking a nickel apiece for them. The fact that he and his wife, both seasoned to hickory stick hardness, had carried water in buckets up from the creek bed to keep their plants alive did not enter into the consideration of the price.

There was also talk of the new house Dee and Finas Fox were building with a big window in the living room and real hardwood floors. The talk lagged and finally there was a long silence. The women's hearts were following their men.

"Mother of God," finally Rosa Rapuzzi blurted out. "Wish we could hear something."

"No news is good news." Mrs. Sadberry was a quiet, meek little woman.

"Bet the damned bastards don't show up." Rosa's Italian blood was boiling. She was not a pacifist.

"I hope they won't." Aunt Ida voiced the sentiment of the group.

"The really smart thing would be to let 'em come on in and go to work. Then send somebody down to blow hell outa 'em. Splatter their guts all over the entry." There was so much hate in Nella's voice that the women frowned and recoiled as though a blind rattler had unwound itself on the porch and was striking out in all directions.

"That don't solve nothing," Aunt Dea said thoughtfully. "Remember what happened at Zeigler. They never could work the mines and the whole town had to move away."

"What's happened?" Aunt Belle stood up and pointed to the woman and children up the street who were leaving their homes and running toward Main Street.

"Lord God!" Cousin Frankie stood with the others, her sightless eyes gazing in the direction of the shouting and commotion. Now she stood alone, for the other women were in the road and on their way to town. Halfway the block they were stopped by John Kirkpatrick who was loping over town with the news.

"Carload of groceries on the siding for us," he panted.

Rosa Rapuzzi stopped suddenly and crossed herself. The lips so recently given to hate and profanity now muttered a fervent "Hail Mary."

"Thought they'd starve us out"—Aunt Dea tossed her head contemptuously in the general direction of the spacious homes of the mine owners and operators—"but God is above the devil every day."

"Be up at the car at four and get enough food for supper. They'll ration it out tomorrow." John Kirkpatrick finished his instructions and passed on down the street.

The fact that groceries would be passed out three hours later did not lessen the speed of the women and children. They wanted to get to the car to touch it, to read the letters on its broad side, to watch the men slide the door back and see the provisions headquarters had sent for the striking miners.

The women carried themselves proudly down the dusty streets. The children jostled each other in fun, stopped to begin a ring game, then abandoned it to chase each other, looking back over their shoulders and squealing, "Tag! You're it!"

Now that the first excitement of the carload of provisions was over, the old apprehension settled again over the women and children. What had happened on the road to Pinkneyville? Uncle George and Rob Jenkins harnessed their surreys and started to find out.

The miners were coming home. They were near the old salt works about two miles out of town. Not a scab had showed up. The men were tired and walked with a slow gait. Their steps quickened when they heard of the provisions. Somebody started "It's a Long Way to Tipperary." Like a column of undefeated soldiers, they marched into town.

The aroma of fried bacon, potatoes, and onions blanketed the whole town.

"Get any rabbits, Papa?" Cecil asked as he swung his feet beneath his chair. Our table did not resemble an international peace parley. Every man sat with his own family. Despair that had camped for weeks at the weather-beaten doors of the miners took her stool and moved on farther down the road.

"Didn't see a cottontail," Dad laughed.

"The food is a godsend." Mother filled a large vegetable dish with steaming hot fried potatoes.

"Charlie Brayfield had a letter from the union headquarters. We'll get a carload a week as long as we're out on strike. Won't be no more kids going around hungry." Dad leaned back in his chair and exhaled deeply.

"Being without money isn't so bad. We never had much, anyway, after the company store got its share. It was knowing that so many people actually didn't have enough to eat—that's what worried me."

"We're home free now," Dad used his favorite baseball

term. "As long as a man's children can eat, he ain't gonna be kicked around."

Evidently the operators were of the same opinion. After the second car of groceries came they called a meeting and agreed to the raise.

Spring and its first robin were gone. In a few months, autumn would be touching the woods with her warm colors of henna, orange, and gold. The extra bedroom would have to wait, for the back grocery bill had to be paid.

The miners whistled and sang as they went to their jobs. The work was still dangerous but they took a fierce pride in outwitting the sharp hooves of the vicious dwarfed mules and eluding the dangerous slides of slate. They were proud, too, because they had won their point. Helen and I didn't mind sleeping in the living room. No room in the world is worth a man's pride.

17. miracle on Smoke Row

If Du Quoin ever had a miracle happen, and what town hasn't had at least one, Martha Morris was it. She lived alone in a little three-room house that defied the ravages of time by her extravagant insistence on a new coat of paint every few years. Her house divided Smoke Row from the white red-light district. It had none of the drabness of the sooty-gray houses of Smoke Row; nor did it slyly wink its eye or beck its finger to the indiscriminate who wanted to "have a little fun." Martha's house, like its owner, minded its own business.

Martha and Cousin Frankie had two things in common. They both took in washings and both "bore a thorn in the flesh." There was nothing wrong with Martha's eyes, but one morning when she awoke, she found that her legs refused to support her body. How long she lay by her bed, trying to bully her feet and legs into accepting their responsibility, she did not know. Her hands ached from the futile clutching of the side rail of the bed as she tried to pull herself up. There was panic in her eyes when she finally crawled to the front door and called for help. Dick and Luella Webb, who lived next door, rushed over and tried to lift her to her feet. After much pulling and straining, they eased Martha's 250 pounds down on the bed.

It was months before Martha was able to drag herself around the house. Rich white folks brought baskets of soiled clothing to be laundered. But Miss Martha did not stand up and wash like other women. She sat sideways at the tub. When she had to move, she planted her massive hands on the most substantial object nearby and pushed herself up. With a half twist of her huge body, she reached for the two stout sticks that she kept within reach to propel herself about the house.

In spite of her physical handicap, she had a pleasant round face; and your look of pity quailed before the merriment in her dark brown eyes. Although someone described her shape as "a sack of cotton with a string tied in the middle," you never thought twice of the cumbersome body. There was too much soul in her face. Her coarse black hair was braided and wrapped coronet fashion around her head.

Aunt Dea, whose rheumatism struck her like chained lightning, said, "Martha's legs done plum' give out from standin' at the wash tub so long." Mother argued that Miss Martha's outward humor was just a cover up to hide inward grief.

A small town does not permit its inhabitants the luxury of past secrets. Even we children knew that Miss Martha had been stricken shortly after she packed Mr. Jack's bag and set it on the front porch. In the early morning hours when he staggered home from Joe Lipe's saloon, he found all the doors locked. Luella and Dick Webb, who had been awakened by Jack's insistent banging, said that he sounded real pitiful. Finally Martha raised the window and yelled for him to get the hell outa there.

Jack had always been a heavy drinker. Without Martha's watchful eye and scolding tongue, he soon degenerated into the town soak. Martha creased and pulled and pressed other folks' clothes while her Jack ambled up and down the streets, his rough-dried shirts soiled, his rusty shoes scuffed and sometimes untied, his wrinkled suits spotted and smelling from too much wear.

Then one Saturday morning it happened. The miracle—I mean. Cousin Frankie and I were returning home from our early morning shopping. We had just rounded the corner of Main Street, where Henry Stoutenberg's cobbler shop was, when we noticed a crowd of women coming up Walnut Street. There were women of all sizes, shapes, and colors.

Cousin Frankie was jerked to a halt as I stopped dead in my tracks. Quick to sense the unusual, she turned her face to me. Her sightless eyes were wide with alarm. "Wha's the matter?" she asked quickly.

"All them women—an' Miss Martha Morris——"

Her quiet voice was controlled but anxious as she interrupted with, "Wha's happened to Martha?"

"She's walkin'!"

"Well?"

I had to make Cousin Frankie see the picture. "I mean like other people. Straight—without sticks—an' there's a crowd——"

"You mean Martha Morris ain't cripple—no mo'?"

I could understand Cousin Frankie's unwillingness to believe. This was something that had to be seen. There was no time for further conversation, for the women were even with us and Martha had grabbed Cousin Frankie's hands and was pumping them up and down as she shouted, unabashed, right out in the middle of the sidewalk:

"Frankie! Frankie!" the deep voice boomed over the quiet street. "The Lord done healed me! Frankie—I can walk!"

And Cousin Frankie, whose spirit could blaze from the tiniest spark of fire, yelled, "Glory!"

I looked from one to the other. Rosa Rapuzzi's swarthy Italian face was enraptured as she mumbled words I could not understand. Over and over, her right hand made the sign of the cross. Shy Anna Molsen, who had come all the way from Poland with her six children to join her husband Alfred, now felt herself a part of the group and she chattered in German to hunchbacked, wizened Tillie Ricks. Mandy Woods, who usually wore a calico dust cap, because, to quote Aunt Dea, "she didn't have a dime's worth of hair," smiled and nodded her bare head in approval as Martha continued to talk.

A little apart, yet following behind the group, Babe and Tommy, two girls from the red-light district, stood close together. Near them, squint-eyed Bessie Tedwell held tight to the hand of her little Rob who limped along, one leg shorter than the other. Here they all stood, faces flushed with excitement, wonder in their eyes.

"You know, Frankie, it's been over ten years since I could walk without my two sticks," Martha testified. "Over ten years, mind you! Well," she paused to take a deep breath, then continued, "this morning I was layin' in bed. I thought about the many things Jesus done when he walked the earth like a natchal man. 'Course I've thought about him often—but I don't know. Today, I seemed to think about him in a special sort of a way. I remembered all the good things he done while he was here. One verse just kep' sayin' itself over an' over to me—'The works that I do, ye shall do also, an' greater works than these shall ye do.'"

With her right hand she patted her breast. "He was

184

talkin' 'bout me, Frankie. He was talkin' to all of us!" Her voice dropped into a low, confidential tone, but its vibrancy increased. "I been prayin' all my life—or leastways, I thought I been. I didn't notice anything different this mornin'—but it musta been different—'cause I ast Jesus—just like I'd ast Luella Webb fo' a cup o' sugar. I said to him, Lord, I wanta walk this mornin'. Jesus, I said, Jesus—please let me walk—this mornin'—right now!"

"Then something seemed to say—yes, that was it," Martha was still trying to fathom the steps that led to her miraculous healing. " 'Cause I never heard a voice, somethin' jus' sorta reasoned inside me. Martha—you can walk, it said. Get up—get up—and walk! I got outa bed—an' stood up." Martha's breath was coming in short gasps. Though the crowd had heard this before, they were still intrigued by this mysterious and glorious thing that had happened on Smoke Row. They looked at each other, smiled, and nodded their approval as Martha finished her story.

"Then I took two or three steps." This part of her story she actually demonstrated by taking a few steps forward, then moving back to her original position. "I was so happy I shouted all over the house. I was halfway off the porch when I remembered my ole walkin' sticks leanin' up against the bed. Luella was the first one who got to me. I tole her what happened an' we started out. I want everybody to know what the Lord done done for me."

And everybody in Du Quoin knew. For Martha, like an inspired prophetess, went all over town, telling the good news, completely forgetting the baskets of white folk's washing that sat on her back porch.

"I'm glad, Martha," Cousin Frankie murmured as they passed on. "I'm so glad!"

All the way home, Cousin Frankie was strangely quiet. She spoke only once and that quite sharply to Hallie Wilburn who observed, "If it was so easy, like she tells it, why didn't it happen to Martha a long time ago?"

"I guess you've answered your own question. Faith is too simple for most of us. It's so simple—we can't understand." Cousin Frankie sighed wearily and passed her hand over her sightless eyes as we continued down the street.

As we pondered the ways of an immutable God, we heard Cousin Frankie's song of supplication that floated over the Bottoms:

> It's me, it's me, Oh Lord,
> Standin' in the need o' prayer.
> It's me, it's me, Oh Lord,
> Standin' in the need o' prayer.
>
> Not mah mother, not mah father,
> But it's me, Oh Lord,
> Standin' in the need o' prayer——

18. balancing the score

Sarah, Mother's youngest sister who lived in Wyoming, sent us a large box of clothing at least twice a year. Aunt Sarah, who often remarked that she wouldn't be caught dead in a cheap dress, loved beautiful materials. When she had tired of a dress or coat she sent it on to Mother to be cut down and made into something for Helen or me. The arrival of a box from Aunt Sarah was always a highlight. We crowded around and had to be pushed back as Mother piled the contents on the library table. Near the bottom of the box was a lovely golden-brown skirt.

"Gee! What's that?" Helen exclaimed.

Mother held the skirt up. It was soft and sleek and shiny as the fur of an ermine.

"It's beautiful," Mother breathed. She shared Aunt Sarah's weakness for expensive materials. "This isn't enough for a dress, but maybe we can get Ruby a jumper skirt out of it. Like it?" She passed the skirt over to me.

"Um-huh," I grunted, as I rubbed my cheek against the softness.

"Then we'll have Mrs. Barber make it up for you. That's real chiffon velvet. Sarah paid a pretty penny for that material."

Mrs. Barber was neat, prim, English, and sewed so neatly you could almost wear the things she made wrong side out. Or at least, that's what Mother said. That is why I was sitting in her sewing room the morning hook-nosed Maggie Daniels yelled across the fence.

"Morning, Mrs. Barber."

"Good morning, Mrs. Daniels."

"Terrible explosion at the mines last night, wasn't it?"

"It certainly was. I'm such a coward. I always dread to see Mr. Barber go to work after an accident."

"Well, it coulda been worse. Woulda too if the men had been down. As it was there was jes twenty mules and a nigger that was killed."

Mrs. Barber turned quickly and looked at me. I averted my glance and suddenly became interested in a calendar just above my head. The beauty of the tulip garden made no impression on me. Inwardly I was seething. I knew how to take care of children who called me names, but what did a ten-year-old girl do with a calloused, slovenly woman who sniffed Copenhagen snuff? Of course I could tell Dad, but he had often said that any man who would hit a woman wasn't a man. Mother, I discounted. She was too much of a lady to come over and mop up the earth with Maggie Daniels. Sometimes having a lady for a mother works a terrible hardship on a youngster.

"But Mr. Webb was such a nice man. I'm thinking about his wife and their four fine children." Mrs. Barber's sympathetic voice was mildly reproving.

"Yes, 'tis a shame. Maybe now the miners'll work harder on that compensation law. Course it won't do the poor devils who get killed any good, but it will keep the wives and children off the poor farm." Maggie Daniels passed on into her house and Mrs. Barber turned away from the window and left the room.

I nodded my head, thankful for the chance to be alone.

balancing the score

At home we had talked of nothing else that morning. The death of Dick Webb was very real to us. Dick had been a big-framed, very dark man. Everybody had liked him. He had not been given to much talk, but he was friendly and always had a ready smile for you. Besides, he was Alice and Buster's dad. The mines didn't work that day.

No one ever knew exactly how Dick Webb met his death. We knew he met it alone. Evidently, he had been transferring powder near the stables, for the explosion which mutilated his body beyond recognition, twisted the iron cars, tore up the tracks, killed twenty mules, and almost demolished the stables.

As I sat quietly awaiting Mrs. Barber's return, I found myself thinking of Dad and Button Cunningham and the perilous job they did every night. Dad had changed from the day shift. He and Button were shot firers at Forester's mine. Suppose some night Dad went back to see why a shot didn't go off, only to find that a kink in the fuse had delayed the explosion.

Dad had once told us about a scary fellow he worked with who was always running out of the room before he had properly lighted the fuse. One night Dad had followed him back into the room to help him. As soon as Dad reached the door, he saw that the fellow had lighted the fuse at first and the powder was ready to go off. As the man started to run, Dad made a flying tackle which carried them back into the room and right under the nose of the shot. Dad pinned the frightened miner to the floor and held him there. The set charge of powder went off with a thunderous roar. The screaming of the man could be heard above the sound of the shot and the rumbling of the coal as it was torn from the vein.

"Chunks of coal as big as that stove flew over our heads," Dad pointed to the big base-burner when he told of the incident several days later. He didn't mention the happening the next morning. That is another unwritten law among miners. If the cold wind of death has breathed down a fellow's neck, he doesn't like to talk about it. You'll get all the details from his partner, or from the fellow who heard the slide and ran to pull the trapped miner out.

Finally, when the coal stopped falling, Dad pulled the fellow to his feet. The scared miner looked at the small mountain of coal that blocked the doorway and collapsed in a dead faint.

But Dick Webb hadn't come back. He would never come back. Never. My eyes became misty as Dad and Dick Webb became intermingled in my thoughts and emotions. Sometimes it seemed that in reality it was Dad who had met death alone, hundreds of feet under the ground.

The door opened and Mrs. Barber came in bearing a beautiful silver-bordered tray.

"You're just in time to have a cup of tea with me. Do you like tea, Ruby?"

"Mother always says growing children should not drink tea or coffee, but she does let us drink sassafras in the spring and iced tea in the summer when it's hot."

"I'm sure she won't mind. I made yours very weak. Now, in England we like our tea strong. The teapot stays on the stove all day." Mrs. Barber was usually a woman of few words, but this morning she seemed especially talkative. "When I've finished with the housework, a cup of tea seems to be just the thing before I get on with my sewing. By the way," she continued as she arranged sugar and cream on the small table, "where did your mother get that material? Why, it's beautiful enough for a coronation robe. You're going to look like a little princess in it."

"Aunt Sarah sent it to me. She lives in Wyoming."

"Your mother said the skirt is to be very full and the silk plaid blouse is to be trimmed in tiny ruffles. My! I'd have given anything to have had a dress like that when I was a little girl."

She sat down and held out a tiny cup. Drinking tea was an experience for me. I was intrigued by the cups. Perfect white figures were raised above a deep blue base.

"These cups are sure pretty, Mrs. Barber."

"Do you like them Ruby?" She seemed a bit surprised.

"I sure do. I never saw such pretty ones before."

"They are very old, Ruby. They belonged to my grandmother. They are Wedgwood. We only use them on special occasions."

I wanted to ask her what occasioned their use on this particular morning, but Mother had warned us against asking questions.

"You see, it is so rarely that I have someone to drink tea with me—I'm celebrating." She answered my unasked question.

We drank our tea leisurely. Mrs. Barber told me that the figures on the cups were Grecian and were scenes from the myths. Finally, the tiny table was pushed out of the way and I stood first on one foot, then on the other as Mrs. Barber cut, fitted, and pinned the jumper skirt into place.

"I have quite a bit of sewing ahead, but I'll try to finish this by next Saturday. Then you may wear it to church on Sunday." Mrs. Barber held the front door open for me. Usually we went out the side door of her house and it didn't occur to me until I was quite a ways down the street that Mrs. Barber had insisted upon the front door on this particular morning.

"All right, Mrs. Barber—and thanks for the tea," I remembered my manners and called back.

"The hinges of hell are made with women's tongues," Uncle Joe Dement often remarked, but early in life I learned that all blanket statements are not one hundred per cent correct.

Something or somebody has a way of balancing the score. As I passed by Maggie Daniels' house, I recalled what she had said about Dick Webb, yet the hard bitter hate would not come again. There was still resentment there, yes, but it was slowly disintegrating in the warm feeling engendered by Mrs. Barber's kindliness. For whereas one woman's tongue had lashed my spirit with a cat-o'-nine tails, another's understanding had healed the wounds. I had no wish to remember the hurt. I thought of the silver-framed tray and the tea served in Wedgwood cups. Again I heard Mrs. Barber's words assuring me—long-legged, skinny, ugly duckling me—that I would look like a princess in my new dress.

19. living is fun

Psychologists tell us that every Negro child grows to adulthood with a sense of frustration. Those psychologists never visited our home. We may have had the frustrations common to childhood—maybe of wanting a classic Grecian nose instead of a short bulbous one. Being black, however, brought no frustration to us. We were colored, but what of it? Black was a mark of distinction, not of condemnation. It was no more to be looked down upon than the almost transparent skin of Polish Anna Molsen; the auburn Jerry Colonna mustache of Jake Druer, our German neighbor; the swarthy complexion of Pete Fantaco, acknowledged mayor of Little Italy; or the frizzly hair of Seymour Levine that protruded from the black skull cap he always wore as he bent over the books at his men's furnishing store.

If anyone had come up to us and even suggested that black people were inferior to people of other racial strains, we would have laughed in their faces. Du Quoin would have been much poorer economically, socially, politically, and spiritually without its Negro citizens. It was our town and we had a sense of belonging to it.

Hand in hand with belonging, with contributing, of course came a sense of satisfaction and enjoyment. During childhood everything was a game. We did not have any chores, as such. I have never known whether this was due to the wise guidance of our parents, or whether we were smart enough to figure out this method of getting things done for ourselves.

"Bet I can get the garbage from St. Nick Hotel before you get the groceries from Forester's," Spud would challenge Cecil. The race was on. Friendly competition was a daily practice.

"Spud, you and Cecil feed the chickens and get in the coal and kindling." Mother would enumerate our duties when we came from school. "Helen you set the table. Ruby, get the tub for your father and put his bath water on." All this was accomplished to the dare of: "Bet I'll beat you through." It was as potent a call to us as was Cortez' cry of "Christo y Santiago," to the motley horde of conquistadors that brought to an end the glory of the Aztecs.

While Helen was wiping off the oilcloth, counting the places at the table, and getting the plates from the cupboard, I was bringing the big No. 3 zinc tub from the back porch and placing it behind the base-burner. Room was made for the copper wash boiler on the back of the kitchen stove, and numerous trips were made to the well to fill it.

"Here chicky, here chicky," Cecil's voice rose and fell as he threw the feed in wide arcs.

"Casey Jones, mounted to the cabin, Casey Jones, orders in his hand——" Spud sang, as he dropped armloads of kindling into the wood box on the porch. Buckets of coal were placed behind both stoves. In a few noisy minutes everything was in apple pie order and we were waiting for Dad to swing down from the miners' coaches, cut across Aunt Belle's yard, and come smiling through the back door.

Competitive work was only a small part of our fun. Every season had its own special type of game, and the long winters did not tax our ingenuity. We teamed up on sides and tacked the heavy comforters Mother made from small woolen squares she salvaged from worn-out coats and pant legs. Sometimes Helen would parch a skillet of field corn. After we had eaten our fill we would divide the remaining grains equally and play "Old Horse," a game in which the participants tried to guess the number of grains of corn in each other's hand.

There were those rare and infrequent nights when Mother went to the White Rose Lodge. If there was a heavy snow upon the ground, we made snow ice cream. We planned this for her night out not because she ever quibbled about the milk we used. Cherry, our cow, gave such an abundance of rich milk that we not only shared it with the neighbors, but we had plenty for butter and cottage cheese and a generous portion of skimmed milk for the hogs. We had snow ice cream when Mother was gone because she was always afraid of us "catching our death of cold," leaving the warmth of the room to run outside and stir the ice cream. Rather than have her wear herself out fretting about our health, therefore, we waited until she and Dad were gone for a few hours.

Aunt Ida, who also went with Mother to lodge meeting, would bring her daughter Blanche to stay with us until they returned home. Blanche was a long lanky girl with a rich cocoa-brown complexion, and her hair, braided and drawn across the top of her head, was held in by two brightly colored plaid ribbon bows.

Because Blanche had no brothers or sisters, she accepted us as such, and her coming not only meant snow ice cream, but impromptu shows as well. In these we were not original. We were perfect mimics as all children are. Whatever the last entertainment we had seen, we repeated for our own enjoyment.

Blanche had taken music lessons from the Catholic sisters, and she was always pianist. Her keyboard was the top of Mother's old Singer machine. As her hands flew over the top of the machine her feet tapped the treadle. Cecil also beat out the time on the bottom of Mother's large tin dishpan, sometimes with his long, tapering fingers, sometimes with two thin sticks which he snatched from the wood box. I carried the melody of the song by wrapping a comb with wax paper and blowing through it. Helen supplied the harmony in the same manner. Hers was a rich Carol Brice contralto voice that was later to be heard in many singing ensembles throughout southern Illinois. Sometimes we harmonized on the old songs we heard Aunt Ida sing, like "Dear Old Girl." Then sometimes we chose the newest song hits, like "Everybody's Doing It" or "Pretty Baby."

The musical numbers were interspersed with jokes, orations, and trips outside to stir the frozen custard from the sides of the pan. We had been introduced to Hawaiian music when the last carnival came to town. Not only had we been captivated by the soft plaintive music of the islands, but we had been intrigued by the movements of the dancers. It was years later that we learned that the hula was danced as part of a religious rite. We had only seen the girls whirling and twisting before the patched and faded sideshow banners.

Now Blanche was bowing and swaying before her improvised keyboard. Helen and I were coaxing the dreamy strains of "Aloha Oe" from our paper-wrapped combs. Slowly from the bedroom came a figure gracefully swaying, bowing, hands waving rhythmically, head tilted to one side.

Mother's rose silk-fringed Spanish shawl was draped about narrow hips that gyrated beneath the soft folds. A lavender feather boa was doing duty for a flower lei around the dark neck. The round eyes that always looked with merriment out upon a world good to live in, gazed demurely toward the flower-figured rug.

"Princess Lakawanii," Cecil shouted.

One look and we were all convulsed with laughter. Tears rolled down Blanche's cheeks. Spud tried to continue his masquerade but the laughter was too much. He staggered back into the bedroom, the rose silk shawl dragging the floor.

By the time Mother and Aunt Ida returned, the ice cream had been eaten, the dishes washed, the younger children put to bed, and we were hard at work with the next day's lessons.

There were other nights when we told riddles as the wind howled through the bare branches of the peach tree that stood outside the north living-room wall. We would start with the smaller children, and the riddles would increase in difficulty as Mother and Dad joined in. We could seldom tell a riddle that was not known by the entire family, but every once in a while Mother or Dad could stump us.

The seasons often indicated the games to be played. In the winter there were sleigh rides and ice skating at Blakesley's old mill pond where baptizings were held in the summer. We pressed the snow in our mittened hands to form little compact balls. We built rotund snowmen that stood for weeks until the sun melted them down or until some mischievous youngster toppled them over.

Spring was the season for kite-making. Kites of all sizes and shapes dotted the sky. Kites whose long tails whipped through the air like winged serpents, octagonal kites with no tails at all, kites as tall as Luther Clary, kites as small as a nickel tablet, simple kites made with two crossed sticks, intricate box kites that stayed aloft in no wind at all.

By May, the ground was thoroughly dry. All over town boys wore out the knees of their overalls as they knelt on the hard ground and shot marbles through a crudely drawn ring. Spud and Cecil kept their prize aggies in a cigar box. The cheaper pee wees, dates, and ordinary glassies were kept in two large coal buckets.

School was out by the last of May. This marked the beginning of berry season. Berry season was fun. Acres of dew berries and black berries grew wild. The whole town frowned upon the farmer who would not let the people come in and pick; so we never concerned ourselves with who owned the land.

We were usually up before Mother and Dad in order to reach the berry fields before the sun was too hot. They lay three or four miles southwest of town and we walked every step of the way, swinging our buckets and singing the school songs we liked best. On the way, we would pass other groups and if they were special friends we would tell them where the nicest berries were to be found.

It was not until summer when twilight lingered hours after sundown on the broad prairies that we played the best-loved games. Morning chores were soon over and the whole day stretched before us. The "marble fever" was over, but you could usually find a game in progress on some side street or in someone's yard. Groups of boys gathered around huge circles and played "peg top." The more timid ones flinched and turned their heads every time the other boys tried to hit their tops. Others salvaged the rubber-tired wheels from broken Christmas wagons and made bullet-headed expresses that raced with incredible speed over Du Quoin's dusty streets.

Sometimes fishing parties were organized. Boards where a bit of moisture may have lingered were overturned by the less energetic who sought the squirming worms to be used as bait. Others took garden forks and turned over the ground, breaking the hard clods and pulling the unwilling worms from their tiny holes. When sufficient worms had been found, they were put in tin cans. Long willow poles were cut, stout string secured, and if there were no regular fishhooks, common dress pins were bent into shape. A crawfish would cling to a pin.

In the morning, we girls played house. Blanche, who even as a child had learned to expect a great deal from life, was always Mrs. Rockefeller. Bessie Sadberry was Mrs. Astor, and Helen was Mrs. Carnegie. A part of anything especially good was saved from our meals for our playhouse. Mrs. Carnegie (Helen) spent a great deal of time visiting. Nellie Sadberry was Blanche's child, and I belonged to Bessie. We used our regular doll dishes which only held enough food for a bird. Mrs. Carnegie usually ate all her food before mealtime, and we could depend upon her dropping in at the Rockefeller or Astor domicile just as we were setting the table.

Somebody has remarked that "God takes care of all fools and babies." I am sure it was true in our case for sometimes we cooked for ourselves. Belonging to the first families of the country, we wanted something extra-special, so we hunted mushrooms. We had a way of telling them from the toadstools, or so we thought. How, I am now at a loss to say, but our luck never ran out. All during our childhood we continued to cook and eat the mushrooms we found in the fields. Even now I shudder to think what might have happened to the country's three wealthiest women and their two little girls if, instead of the harmless mushrooms, we had gathered the poisonous toadstools.

Afternoons, under the shade of the tall poplars in Horn's pasture, we played ring games. Sometimes the boys would join us. Sometimes they looked down their noses at us and told us to "go south." They were always ready to play kick the can, frog in the middle, or chickany, chickany, crany crow, however, because these were action games.

We played ball after supper. When there were no meetings of importance, Dad, Uncle Robert, Uncle Lewis, Ernest Smith, Big Head, Charlie Molsen, and even Duza from the North End, would join us. They were some of the best ballplayers in town. We played in the middle of the road in front of our house. Those who were not participating would sit on their porches and root for their favorites. The men took the places of importance on each team and we loitered in the field while the pitchers battled it out. Sometimes the batter knocked a sizzling grounder. A quick interception by Big Head, who always played shortstop, and the ball speeding to Duza Powers on first base meant a sure out.

No matter how long twilight lingered, it was finally pushed gently aside. The tall elms, the spires of the Catholic church, and the breast-shaped dome of the post office were now indiscernible at a distance. Night wore a soft dress of black velvet, and the hundreds of glowworms with their phosphorus sacks were her rhinestones and sequins.

From a distance you might hear someone yell "cabbage and cornbread" or "red-hot skillet," and you knew that children were playing run, sheep, run. The yells were signals from the leaders for the sheep either to stay hidden or to make a break for home.

Saturday nights the German and Polish people had their own dances. Albert Beutcher had made a small pavilion under his grape arbor. Here they would gather at dusk. A small keg of beer was put on tap. The shelf above it was filled with imported stein mugs. Frank Molsen who played the violin never dreamed that years later his son Yeets would play first violin with the Chicago Symphony Orchestra. The accordion was the only other instrument that was used. We always stood by the fence and watched until we were called home. We heard the music of Strauss and Liszt, quaint Bohemian folk songs that set the older people among the familiar lands of their childhood. The younger Polish and German children stood outside with us and watched. They were learning the fox trot and the bunny hug.

Sometimes we would ask permission to go up to Little Italy and watch the Italians dance. They were by far the better dancers. They waltzed more smoothly and with more grace than did their neighbors, and there was a courtliness about the Italians that was missing in the German and Polish men.

Sometimes when I look at some of the nervous, frustrated children of today with their radio crime programs, their exposure to pseudopsychological pictures and the insecurity of broken homes, I like to think back on my childhood in Du Quoin. Our simple games, the quiet playtimes, were enjoyed by all. We didn't need five murders in ten minutes on the radio to give us a thrill. Eluding the witch in chickany, chickany, crany crow, receiving a red and white stick of peppermint candy, being chosen to play whip cracker, or appointed a leader in children I call you, was thrill enough.

Life was as gay as a gypsy dance, and the whole world was garlanded in roses. Childhood was a time of growing and fun, and having fun was not related to the color of one's skin.

20. a bishop visits our city

At first glance it seemed that the Baptists had a corner on the religious market in Du Quoin. They boasted of four churches: rebuilt Mt. Zion, pastored by Lija Holmes; Free Will Baptist, pastored by Grandpa Berkley; Mt. Olive, presided over by Elder Winston; and a sprawling, squawking hybrid, St. Paul, that had gathered its members from dissatisfied factions of all three.

The African Methodist Episcopal Zion Church carried the banner of John Wesley proudly and alone. It needed no sister church to bolster its morale. Its offerings exceeded the combined collections of its four rivals. Come blizzard, stifling heat, or hail storm, you would always find Ottoway and Mary Scott, Sarah and Joe Love, John and Belle Kirkpatrick, the Mason, Peters, and Berkley clans in their family pews on Sunday morning.

Strangely enough, this was the only church to which the fancy women of our town seemed to feel free to come. Beautifully dressed but decorous, these girls from North Oak and South Division streets quietly entered the church almost in a body and sat throughout each Sunday morning service.

"Maybe it's all right," Cousin Dora, who was Baptist, said skeptically one day when the topic came up for discussion, "but everybody knows how they get their money."

Mother looked at Cousin Dora, then nodded her head toward us.

"Oh Sophia, don't be such a prude. These children ain't no fools. Everybody in town knows what everybody else does. They probably know more about Rena and Hallie and Katie than we do."

"Just the same, neither Braxton or I talk about people before the children."

And that was the truth. The uncomplimentary things we learned about the people of Du Quoin were never learned at home. They were learned on the schoolground, or on our way to the company store, or when visiting some of our friends.

Dad had been quietly figuring how many entry feet he had cut that fortnight. Evidently he had heard Cousin Dora's remarks for as he put his small notebook in his inside coat pocket, he said slowly, "I guess we look at people different from God."

"Well, I don't know. The Bible makes it pretty plain about some things." Cousin Dora defended her righteous stand.

"Yes, it does. I was just thinking when they brought one of these same women to Jesus. He told the people who were accusing her, 'Let him that is without sin cast the first stone.' I've heard people say that nobody throwed a rock. Then one time when I was a little boy I heard another preacher say that an old hypocrite raised his hand to throw a stone and his hand become paralyzed and the Lord had to stop and heal him. But I ain't never found that in the Bible, though I've read the gospels many a time."

"Braxton, you ain't trying to say that one sin is as big as another."

"I never found yet in the Bible where Jesus said, 'you can do this 'cause it's just a little sin, but don't do that 'cause it's a great big sin.' He jes lumps 'em all together and says, 'Don't lie; don't kill; don't steal.' "

"Well, I can see why they go to your church, if the pastor and the trustees feel like you do. I wish they'd have the brass to stick their noses in St. Paul one Sunday. Wouldn't Rev. Wright get them told?"

"Rev. Wright? That old chippy-chasing devil ain't as good as an honest prostitute."

"Braxton!" Mother's shrill voice put an end to Dad's tirade. Smugness always did something to Dad. He wanted to tear the mask off and let people see the conceit and deceit it usually covered.

But we had heard a few things about Rev. Wright too; so we snickered. Cousin Dora got so mad you could fry an egg on her head.

Dad's anger reminded me of our rains in April. It passed quickly. He was now thoroughly ashamed of himself. He mumbled something indistinct in an apologetic tone and left the room.

In a few minutes we heard him outside, his sonorous voice lifted in song:

> "Shine on me, shine on me,
>   Let the light from the lighthouse
>   Shine on me——"

But despite denominational differences, the occasional visit of any religious dignitary would weld all forces into one group.

It was cold enough to freeze the howl in a hound dog's throat the night Bishop George W. Blackwell preached at our church. Ordinarily, people wouldn't stick their heads out of doors in such weather; that is, grown people. Of course, no matter how low the temperature dropped, there were always a few foolish children who ran back and forth from the house to the snowdrift to stir the little cups of milk, sugar, and vanilla that they proudly called "snow ice cream."

With mittens, mufflers, stocking caps, fleece-lined coats and leggings, we strode along in the wake of Mother and Dad. I always made it a point to walk behind Dad, for no matter how cold the weather, his long overcoat was always open and made a perfect windbreak as it billowed out in the biting air.

"Watch out there." Dad pointed to a framed admonition that hung on the west wall. In boldface type it said, "A REVERENT SILENCE IS REQUESTED." Immediately we quieted down.

Pushing open the swinging doors, we entered the auditorium. Ottoway Scott was throwing a scuttle of coal in the blazing base-burner. Henry Mason, Button Cunningham, Levi and Eliza Robinson were warming themselves at a respectful distance. Aunt Tad and her sister, Mary Scott, along with Sarah and Joe Love were already in their pews.

Rosetta Froner and her mother, Elizabeth Barnett, Larkie and Dovey Person, Dan and Sally Hawkins, led the Baptist contingent. They were followed by a group of white people who had evidently read of Bishop Blackwell's visit in our local paper, the Du Quoin *Evening Call*. It never occurred to me during the whole of my childhood that there was anything unusual in the way the *Call* recorded all the nice things that happened among the Negroes. If something slightly on the sordid side happened, we didn't look for a story on it in the *Call*.

"You couldn't pay Gus Essick to put that mess in his paper," Elizabeth would say. Even before Johnny Mercer wrote it, Gus Essick believed in "accentuation of the positive."

There was no processional by the choir. As the members came in, they greeted their friends, then found their seats in the choir stand to the left of the pulpit. Annie Robinson, the organist, marked her places and whispered back and forth to Obie and Ellen Huddleston, Sadie Vessel, and Uncle Robert. Other members came in and proudly took their seats in the choir loft.

The pews were all full now and the men had gone next door to Carrie Saunder's house and borrowed all her straight chairs. They had also borrowed chairs from Aunt Judith's house across the road.

We saw Annie Robinson look toward the entrance; then she turned quickly to her keyboard and played the introduction:

Holy, holy, holy, Lord God Almighty,
Early in the morning our song shall rise to Thee;

The entire congregation rose and sang with the choir. Down the aisle came Reverend S. D. Davis, our pastor. At his side walked a medium-sized, brown-skinned man in a frock-tail coat. There was a gentleness about his features in spite of serious countenance. His black, slightly crinkly hair was parted on one side. You scarcely noticed his facial features, though you were inclined to dismiss them as "nice," but you were held by the eyes that seemed to burn with an inner mystic flame. I knew this was Bishop Blackwell. Elder Pete Thompson, our local preacher, and Rev. Brockett of the St. Paul Baptist Church followed them through the chair-filled aisle.

As they reached the rostrum, Bishop Blackwell stopped to shake hands with Father Simmons, who always sat in a place of honor near the pulpit. Sometimes we bought mustard greens from Father Simmons. Mother always said he was the most exact man in the world.

"He wouldn't cheat you out of a penny, but he wouldn't give you a leaf over what you had coming to you," was the way she described his sales transactions.

Now the ministers stood facing the congregation and joined in the singing:

> All Thy works shall praise Thy name
> In earth, and sky, and sea——

Rev. Brockett, in precise Bostonian accent, read the Scriptures. He was entirely too cultured for the proletariat of Du Quoin. When the Brocketts first came there, Mrs. Brockett held a few informal teas at home where she presided over an antique silver service, dressed in long black taffeta skirts and dainty white voile shirtwaists with choker necks stiffened with whalebone. All the women attended but frowned on the scanty menu. Tea and wafers were not for women who did large washings by hand and who had to carry their water perhaps half a block. Rev. Brockett leveled off one side of their parsonage yard and put up a tennis net. Aunt Belle and some of the more zealous ones tried to master the intricacies of the game but the little white ball had the most uncomfortable habit of bouncing where the women were not. Tennis might be all right for the young and foolish, but soon Aunt Belle decided that she wasn't young any more; so somebody substituted a croquet set.

Tonight, Rev. Brockett, who had tried to gear his intellectual prowess to Du Quoin's nonchalance, felt more at home. He was on the same platform with a man who spoke his own language. While Bishop Blackwell did not have a Bostonian accent, he had been to Boston. Doubtless Rev. Brockett understood fully the emotion that gripped the heart of the doctor when a young reporter found him in the heart of an African jungle and said in greeting, "Dr. Livingston, I presume." Rev. Brockett's voice was usually as cold as it was correct. Tonight, slightly colored by a suggestion of emotion, it was warm and fluid.

Elder Pete Thompson added a little bit more to his usual prayer, which always included, "We thank Thee that we are in a Bible land and a gospel country." The choir romped home on the anthem, "Oh How Lovely is Zion," and the church was in fine spiritual mettle when Rev. Davis rose to introduce the guest of honor. As a gracious host he welcomed the overflowing church, good-naturedly chiding some of the members who came to church only on Easter and Christmas.

Rev. Davis employed eloquence without verbosity. He was of the people but slightly above them. He often used wit but never resorted to commonness. Zion Church was proud of her pastor that night. His introduction of the bishop was beautiful in its simplicity.

As the bishop advanced to the pulpit, the entire congregation rose to its feet in token of respect. For us the ninth chapter of Isaiah became alive and glowed in our hearts like burning coals on an altar:

"For unto us a child is born, unto us a son is given: and the government shall be upon his shoulder: and his name shall be called Wonderful, Counselor, The mighty God, The everlasting Father, The Prince of Peace. Of the increase of his government and peace there shall be no end, upon the throne of David, and upon his kingdom, to order it, and to establish it with judgment and with justice from henceforth even for ever."

Bishop Blackwell did not bob and weave about the pulpit like a punch-drunk prize fighter. He did not rant and rave like Rev. Belton, whom Uncle Robert described as "always hollering like he thought God was a long ways off." He did not use big words like Algie Bradley, who would never use a one-syllable word if he could dig up a four-syllable one.

The sonorous, well-modulated voice soothed and comforted us. He talked not so much about the littleness of man as he did about the bigness of God. Man, made in God's likeness, therefore took on His attributes, His stature, and His vision. He spoke with authority about the permanence of God's kingdom, the equity of His justice, and the inevitableness of His judgment.

"That man's got more than a speaking acquaintance with Jesus," Dad summed it up as we walked home after the meeting.

But while he was speaking, you did not stop to analyze the source of his power. You knew beyond the slightest shadow of a doubt that this was the God you could wholly surrender to. For a few moments you understood the passion that motivated the lives of the first century Christians, who thanked God that they were accounted worthy to suffer for His name's sake.

He talked at length about this wonder-God, this classless God, who loved Eli George with his black face and bloodshot eyes as much as he did Ben Tracy, who lived in a mansion and drove the finest pair of bays in town. He introduced us to an understanding God who "knew our frame and remembered that we were dust." Finally he told us of the all-loving God, whose supreme sacrifice dwarfed all our human suffering.

In closing, he challenged man's ethics, his faulty vision, his imperfect judgment, his flagrant miscarriage of justice by pointing to the perfection of God's kingdom. With prophetic clearness, his eloquent voice closed his sermon with this song of affirmation:

> Jesus shall reign where e'er the sun
> Does his successive journeys run;
> His kingdom spread from shore to shore,
> Till moon shall wax and wane no more.
>
> Blessings abound where e'er He reigns,
> The prisoner leaps to lose his chains,
> The weary find eternal rest,
> And all the sons of want are blest.

He motioned for the congregation to stand and he blessed us as a father, going on a long journey, might bless his children.

"Let us all shake hands before we separate and go to our homes. Will some one lead us in a song?" Rev. Davis stepped to the front of the rostrum.

Annie Robinson started turning the pages of her songbook, but before she had found her special number, even before John Kirkpatrick's rolling bass could start "I Am Bound For the Promised Land," or Uncle Robert's wavering tenor could raise "I Gave My Life For Thee," Dad had turned to shake hands with an occupant in the next aisle and was leading the church in:

> In Thy cleft, oh Rock of Ages, Hide Thou me,
> When the fitful tempest rages, Hide Thou me——

Everybody was singing and shaking hands. There were no more Methodists, Baptists, white folks, or colored folks. You were vaguely conscious of Ellen Huddleston's beautiful contralto voice harmoniously threaded into the web of song. Dad's voice could be distinctly heard above the crowd:

> In the sight of Jordan's billow,
> Let Thy bosom be my pillow,
> Hide me, oh, Thou Rock of Ages,
> Safe in Thee.

We knew that you had only to reach out your hand to touch the kingdom of God; for its glory, majesty, and power enveloped us in one radiant, all-inclusive circle of brotherhood.

21. Davis' mine goes on a rampage

The whistle on the engine house at Old Davis' mine had gone crazy and was screaming its head off.

It interrupted the lessons at Lincoln School where Miss Emma Tate was screeching at Earl Simmons, "No! No! No! Illinois is not bounded on the east by Maryland. Here is Maryland, 'way over there." She had just raised her pointer to pierce the heart of Maryland on the map, when the whistle started.

There was something ominous in the continued irregular sound. The mine whistles were as familiar to us as our mother's voice. We heard them night and morning. Two long blasts for work—a few short ones, no work.

The children looked about the room at each other, then back to their teacher. Miss Tate had put the pointer in the chalk rack and now sat limply at her desk. Evidently she had heard it before, for her quiet voice was filled with leashed terror as she tried to say calmly, "Children, I believe something has gone wrong at the mines."

Mrs. Anderson, looking like the model for a dainty French miniature, came from across the hall. She and Miss Tate whispered together. In a few minutes they were joined by William Barnett and Professor Taborn, the principal.

"Children," Miss Tate announced when she turned back into the room, "Professor Taborn has decided that you may be excused for the day. You are to go straight home, and

213

stay there," she emphasized. "No matter what you hear,
do not go out to the mines. It is no place for children. Now
remember, do not go out to the mines! Class excused."

We rushed home, stopping to inquire about the explosion of everyone we met.

"Yes, there was an explosion at Davis' mine."

"No, nobody knew what had caused it."

"No, nobody knew who was killed. Maybe nobody. A
smart miner knew ways to protect himself."

"Of course, if it all happened so suddenly the men did
not have time— Run along, children, run along home. You
ask too many questions."

Mother was ironing a shirt for Dad when we rushed into
our house.

"Yes, I heard about the explosion. No, there wasn't anything the women could do—but wait. Yes, of course—pray,
just wait and pray. No, Dad didn't work at Davis' mine, but
Uncle Robert did. No. No, I'm not going out to the mine.
I'm going up to sit with Ida. Her heart's been acting up
since she heard about the explosion. Yes, Aunt Belle and
Aunt Tad are going out to the mine. Sure they are going
to walk. Yes, Aunt Belle has a horse and buggy, but what
good are they if Belle can't hitch or drive Old Nellie. No,
you can't go out to the mine."

"Miss Anderson told us——" Cecil began, but a sharp
kick from Spud silenced him.

"I don't want to go." Helen was no good in an emer-
gency. " 'Spose they bring some of the men up all bloody
and——"

"Hush, Helen," Mother interrupted.

"Maybe I can run and get some water for somebody,
Mama. Please let me go. I'd keep out of the way," Spud
pleaded.

"Yes, Mama, me and Spud could run fast. Please let us go."

"If Ruby and Spud go, I wanna go too," Cecil whined.

"I said no!" Mother set the iron down on the board so hard it rattled the dishes in the tall cupboard that stood against the east wall.

"You're too little, Cecil. Ain't he too little, Mama?" Spud did not want Cecil along.

"It's no place for children." We knew Mother was weakening.

"Aw, Mama, we can take care of ourselves. Can't we, Ruby?" Spud was persistent.

"Well, Spud, I guess maybe you and Ruby can go. Cecil, you'd better stay here. You children better stay with Tad and Belle too, and for heaven's sake, keep out of the way of the workers when you get out to the mine."

We shot across the road and soon caught up with Aunt Belle and Aunt Tad, Uncle Robert's wife. From every direction people were converging on the road that led to Davis' mine. For a while we walked sedately behind the older folks. To break the monotony we tried stepping in their tracks or mimicking Old Man Leggins, whose right leg was shorter than his left.

In her nervousness, Aunt Belle was fanning the ruffled tail of her Paisley basque. Ordinarily Aunt Tad was a very talkative woman. Now she walked along silently, not even hearing the few questions Aunt Belle asked her. Cecilia Randall, who joined them at the railroad tracks, wore a red and white polka-dot bonnet. Her long ruffled dress swept the light gray dust in the road.

Little by little we moved past Aunt Belle and Aunt Tad and were soon out in front of the crowd. When we reached the mine, many of the workers stood about. The cage was lifting the men as fast as it could drop to the bottom and be loaded. Uncle George, the town constable, had assumed control and had stretched a rope to keep the crowds away from the shaft.

As the cage bolted to the surface a small stream of men scrambled off.

"Hans," a Polish woman screamed. The man emerged from the group of miners and ran to the woman behind the rope.

"How do they know 'em?" I questioned Spud. "They're all as black as the ace of spades."

"Search me," Spud shrugged his shoulders.

"Maybe if you love somebody——" I began.

"Peanuts," Spud scoffed. "You been reading too many of them ten-cent novels. What happened, Uncle George?" Spud yelled to Uncle George as he came near.

"Don't know for certain, but it looks like some green-horn walked into a big gas pocket," Uncle George muttered with contempt. "There's an unsealed vein of coal—been burning for God only knows how long. The explosion blocked off the north entry and unless somebody gets in there and puts that fire out, the men back there will be gonners. Course, if the fools have sense enough to save their strength, or just lay down til we work through to 'em, they should be all right. That is if the black damp don't get to 'em before we do."

"You going back down there?" Spud's eyes were filled with wonder. Mine were filled with fear.

"Sure, we're just waiting to get the men off the bottom." Uncle George passed on down the line giving information, assurance, and warning as it was needed.

"Wonder who did it?" I said more to myself than to Spud.

"Whoever he was, bet he don't do it no more. He's a gonner."

"Bet Dad wouldn't a done a thing like that."

" 'Course not, or no other miner with a lick of sense." Spud shared the old miners' contempt for a novice. The safety of so many men depended on the knowledge of one.

A miner had to tell by the flicker of his carbide light, the amount of gas in the entry or in his room. He had to know when to put a prop under hanging sheets of coal. He had to know how to set his powder to keep the shot firer from being blown to bits when he lighted the fuses at night.

Aunt Belle and Aunt Tad had reached the mine by this time.

"George," Aunt Belle's voice carried across the field of anxious watchers.

Uncle George whirled and ran to where Aunt Belle stood jumping up and down like a rubber ball. He took her in his arms and held her tightly. She clung to him and two tiny tears squeezed themselves through her tightly closed eyelids.

"Gee, Spud, I didn't know Uncle George and Aunt Belle were in love with each other."

"For criminey sakes, girls can say some of the darndest things." Spud was thoroughly disgusted with me. I didn't want him to class me with other girls. He could get me to do anything by prefacing his request with, "You know, Ruby, you ain't like other girls." One day someone told us that if a girl kissed her elbow she would be instantly changed into a boy. Many times after that I nearly twisted my arm out of socket as Spud raised my elbow and Cecil pushed my head toward it, trying to bring this magical change to pass.

"Where's Robert?" Aunt Tad pulled impatiently at Uncle George's worn coat sleeve.

"He hadn't come up a little while ago," Uncle George drew away from Aunt Belle and started back toward the shaft. "He may be out now."

We looked toward the shaft. There was renewed activity but no men were being brought to the top. A few men were running about, jerking levers, banging on iron pipes, yelling at each other.

"That son of a bitchin' cage is stuck on the bottom!" a man's angry voice yelled.

We were not shocked by the man's words; we were shocked by the import of his news. With this speedy means of escape cut off, the men now faced a long, hard climb up the ladder which afforded the only other outlet.

"But Robert can't climb the ladder," Aunt Tad whispered mournfully. "He never could climb the ladder." Miners' asthma would make him short of breath.

"They'll probably have the cage fixed in no time," Uncle George tried to comfort her.

Minutes passed and still the men worked frantically to release the cage. A slow freight passed and miners from Forester's and Eaton's swung themselves off the cars. Dad was one of the first men we saw.

"Dad," Spud ran yelling. "The cage is broke and Uncle Robert is still down in the mines. Aunt Tad said he can't climb the ladder."

"I know it. That's why I hurried over," Dad stated simply.

"But you ain't going down there?" Spud looked into Dad's face.

"I sure am. Robert will be waiting for me at the foot of the ladder. I ain't never failed him yet, Spud." Dad play-

218

fully slapped Spud on the backsides, walked over, signed a slip to absolve the mine owners from blame for any injury he might receive, and walked briskly to the entrance of the pit.

The ladder, in reality, was a circular, narrow stairway that wound corkscrew fashion down into the bowels of the earth to where the men worked. A narrow landing was spaced about every twenty-five feet. Dad climbed over the boxed edge and soon his tiny light was lost in the gaping darkness.

The first man up the ladder was Angelo Sandetta. A shout of welcome hailed him as his flickering light rose out of the blackness. Eager hands reached to assist him up the last few steps.

"Damn!" he exclaimed, as he smiled to the people about him. "The old sun looks damned good."

Frank Schwartz and George Parsons were close behind him. There was a slight lull and then it seemed that the men were being hoisted on an escalator, so closely did they follow one another.

John Kirkpatrick was a slow moving individual. He never seemed to be in a hurry about anything. Finally when he appeared we grew apprehensive. Was Uncle Robert at the foot of the ladder waiting for Dad, or was he trapped with the others in the north entry?

"See anything of Papa and Uncle Robert, Mr. Kirkpatrick?" Spud asked, as soon as John shuffled near enough to hear him.

A strange and terrifying silence settled over the crowd that pushed impatiently against the ropes. John's answer was slow in coming. He was still breathing heavily from the long, hard climb.

"I reckon miner's asthma done took all the wind out of me and Robert's sails, but he's a-coming. He an' Braxton ain't far behind. Your Uncle Robert had to stop and rest for quite a spell."

As one man, the crowd emitted a sigh of relief and the eyes, fearful and apprehensive, became bright with hope.

"You know," someone quite close remarked, "if there ever was a Damon and Pythias, it's Brax and Robert."

"What's Damon and Pythias?" Spud whispered.

"Didn't you go to the Knights of Pythias turnout?" I asked.

"Sure, but what's that got to do with Dad and Uncle Robert?"

"Nothing, only that's all they ever preach about."

"Well, what do they preach about?"

"Damon and Pythias, silly."

"That's what I'm asking you. What did they ever do?"

"Nothing, only one of them was supposed to get hung or shot or something, but he wanted to go home and see his wife and children; so the friend agreed to take his place and be killed if the other didn't come back," I rattled off.

"Gee whiz. You don't mean the other guy was willing to be killed just so his friend could go tell his wife and children good-by?"

"Sure."

"Well, if you ask me, I think he was nuts, just plain nuts."

"I think he was noble."

"Noble—huh," Spud snorted his contempt. "Did the other guy get back in time?"

"I don't remember, but I think he did."

"You think he did? That don't do the poor guy no good if he didn't. When did this happen, anyway?"

"Ages ago."

'Shucks. I thought it just happened. Folks got better sense now'days." Youth is forever contemptuous of old things.

"But look what Dad is doing," I challenged.

"Oh, that's different. Somebody had to go down and walk up with Uncle Robert."

The mere mention of Uncle Robert's name again seemed to call him into being. As we looked at the mouth of the ladder, both Dad and Uncle Robert appeared at the surface. They were patted on the back, mauled, and knocked about considerably. Aunt Tad pushed her way through the crowd of rough, yet tender men, and nearly kissed all the coal dust off Uncle Robert's face.

No one knew exactly what started it, but now the cage was brought slowly to the top of the shaft. It was lowered and raised a few times to try it, then a group of volunteers and examiners went down into the mine.

As the men sat around, they speculated upon the damage done to the north entry. Sacks of Bull Durham were passed to those expert at rolling their own. The men watched as Sonny McNary sent a little smoke ring through one that had expanded. Past explosions at Dowell and Old Enterprise were retold. Nobody thought of the food in the dinner pails.

The women walked around absent-mindedly greeting each other two or three times without remembering they had spoken before.

Finally word went through the crowd that the bodies of the dead miners were being brought to the top. One soiled piece of canvas covered all that was mortal of Tom Wheaton, a laughing Irishman; of Henry Burger, a quiet, methodical German; and of Mose Jarrett, a Negro whose melodious voice had filled the north entry with song.

Anxiety gave way to genuine grief. A single scream rose above the wailing of the women and children.

"No! No! No!" Tom Wheaton's wife moaned as she tried to break from the arms of the friends who sought to comfort her.

Anna Burger covered her face with her blue and white checked apron and held her two children close to her heart. She was trying to control the trembling but the muffled sobs shook her as she swayed to and fro.

Amanda Jarrett, unmindful of the supporting arms of her friends, seemed to be fulfilling her last duty to Mose. She was presenting her son to the great Judge of all men.

"He was always a good boy, dear Jesus. He never give me a minute's worry. Now he's coming home to you. Open wide the doors of your kingdom and let my child in." Then as the enormity of her loss slowly dawned in her consciousness, tears gushed from her eyes like water from a fountain. "But Jesus, he's all I've got—all in the world I've got—all in the world——"

Together these three men had worked. Together they had died. Now the people mourned together as though in death they had become symbolic of the oneness of all humanity.

The men took big hunks out of their Old Star tobacco, and spat contemptuously toward the mine shaft.

"Damned dirty deathtrap," John Olinski muttered, as he ground a lump of coal to powder beneath his heavy boot.

22. *Dad converts a socialist—almost*

As I think of it now, Brick Taylor was an idealist. That wasn't what Dad called him when they had a big argument about politics one day. Dad called him a wall-eyed, limber-legged ole fool.

Dad followed the Republican party with a blind loyalty, but he liked to argue with Brick who was a darned good coal digger even though he wore an I.W.W. button. Brick was nobody's fool. Whenever he had a point to make he always started out by using the subtle art of flattery. Dad was a sucker for this type of bait—up to a point.

Brick usually dropped around after supper. We children enjoyed the arguments as much or more than Brick and Dad did.

"Mr. Berkley, I'm surprised at you." Brick's tone was a mixture of shocked horror and unbelief.

"You're surprised at what?" Dad asked bluntly.

"You were active in helping raise funds for Eugene Debs."

"Sure, he was a great man." Dad defended.

"You fought for a lot of laws that made the mines safer, when you were chairman of the pit committee."

"Well, a man don't take his life in his hands every time he goes down on the cage now," Dad admitted.

"An' you fought for miner's compensation and also adequate protection for the wives and children in case of death."

"Anybody would have done that."

"But anybody didn't. You had the vision to fight for those reforms. That's what I've been trying to tell you. All along you've shown yourself to be a socialist of the first water. You are one of our strongest leaders. Then why don't you join our ranks?"

"I'd never be a I.W.W. I've worked all my life."

"So have I." Brick defended. "That 'I Won't Work' label is something people say to ridicule us. You should know something about name calling."

"People don't call me names, Brick Taylor. Leastways, not to my face. What a man is coward enough to say behind my back I don' consider."

"You're right," Brick agreed. "You're right on so many issues. That's why we want you on our side."

"I am on your side. I'm on every workingman's side. Understand me, I ain't down on the rich man, if he's square with his men. I've fought some of the operators to a standstill because I know they ain't got no heart for the worker, but a fair operator gets my o.k. any day."

"I still say we ought to all stick together."

"Why can't I do as much good for the workingman as a Republican?" Dad wanted to know. "Lincoln was a Republican."

"Yes, but the Republican party hasn't produced but one Lincoln," Brick reminded Dad.

"It hasn't needed but one Lincoln."

"Do you know anything about the principles of socialism?" Brick asked.

"Only what I heard from Chester Dunlap, but I know

enough to know that a lot of high-sounding words don't make a man morally good. Maybe I got off on the wrong foot with socialism. I don't know. You can be the judge.

"Chester Dunlap was always readin' an' talkin' about dividin' up the money; so everybody could have an equal share. I kept tellin' him if he did, in two or three years the same fellows would have it all back; the rest would be workin' for wages, and tramps would still be askin' for handouts. You can't pass a law and make everybody decent, or honest, or thrifty."

I remembered the day when Chester came to Dad with a proposition. They could get a fine Poland-China sow dirt cheap. He knew a fellow who was moving from the country and this was the only pig he had left. They talked it over and Chester said he'd like to go partners on it; only he didn't have the money right then for his half of the hog, nor did he have any place to put it.

"I got plenty of corn stored up, and the five dollars won't break me," Dad assured him. That afternoon they went out in the country and got the hog.

On payday Dad asked Chester for his two dollars and a half. Chester always had a good excuse for not paying. Dad got the hog in early fall. By December she was so fat she could hardly walk around the pen. She was corn-fed and as solid as a dollar.

Dad met Chester uptown one Saturday night. "Chester, that hog is about ready to kill. Come over the first day the mines don't work, and we'll butcher her."

"Brack," Chester rubbed his chin with his thumb and forefinger. "You know I been thinking. Maybe we shouldn't kill that sow."

"Not kill the sow? Man, are you crazy?"

"Well, not exactly. That sow is a thoroughbred Poland-China, you know, and her pigs would bring a good price."

"You remember, Chester," Dad reminded him, "you never paid me for your half of that hog. You never bought her a mouthful of feed. By rights you ain't got no part in the hog."

"Brack, we agreed to share and share alike. One for all and all for one. That's the first rule of socialism."

"Listen, that sounds all right, but that talk didn't put one pound of fat on that hog. I paid my five dollars for her. I feed her my good field corn. I coulda ground it up and feed it to Sophia's chickens and turkeys."

"And you'll never regret it, my friend, never. Come on in and have a beer and let's talk this thing over. We want to act in the best interest of all, you know."

Dad followed Chester back into the saloon. Lee Smith pushed a couple of glasses of beer across the counter. As they drank Chester made plans.

"Now, Brack, you figure out how much the feed cost you. Figure it down to the last grain of corn. I owe two and a half on the initial price of the hog, but Brack, I'm still of the opinion that we should not kill her. I intend to raise off my half. Maybe she'll have eleven pigs. That will be five and a half pigs for each one of us. I'll settle up everything on payday, Brack. Of course, I can't pay you for the care, but I'd do the same for you, and you know it, don't you, Brack?"

Dad did not answer that question, but as he left, he delivered an ultimatum.

"Chester, I don't believe in playing about money. I ain't gonna look you up payday, but if you mean right, you'll bring me the money you owe. I ain't charging you for taking care of the hog."

226

"I'll see you, Brack."

Payday came, but no Chester. The next morning Dad was up early, heating huge tubs of boiling water. By noon the Poland-China hog had been killed, scalded, scraped, and cleaned. Dad found Chester in the midst of a friendly argument in front of John Simmon's pool hall. Chester seemed to lose his zest for argument when Dad came up.

"Go along, Riley," he said playfully to Riley Lane, "Brack and I got to talk business. We aim to get ahead. We went partners on a thoroughbred Poland-China sow, didn't we, Brack? We gonna raise off of her, ain't we, Brack?"

Dad nodded his head.

"You know them Poland-China brood sows," Chester continued, "they just liable to come up with a litter of eleven or twelve pigs. That means we'd have five or six pigs apiece. That ain't bad for a five-dollar investment, is it?"

Chester was smiling broadly and started to put his hand on Dad's shoulder. The look in Dad's eye must have arrested him. His hand stopped in midair, then dropped limply to his side.

"Chester," Dad's voice had a bit of an edge on it, "I done killed and cleaned that sow. Tonight I'm going to cut my half up and salt it down. I'll leave your half up there for you to raise off—that is, if you still want to."

Brick Taylor did not stay long after the story of Chester Dunlap was finished. His voice had lost a great deal of its conviction but he still tried to come to the defense of his political brother by saying weakly as he passed out the door, "A very unusual fellow, Mr. Berkley—a most unusual fellow."

23. *our pioneers in race relations*

I don't know how old I was when I discovered that the brotherhood of men we talk so glibly about is already an accepted fact on the lowest and highest levels of life. The only people unwilling to concede its urgency and practicability belong to the great respectable middle class and the powers that rule at the expense of divided peoples. Du Quoin was full of examples.

Grandmother Berkley organized the first union of domestic workers when Dad was just a little shaver. They were asking the unheard-of sum of twenty-five cents per hour for housework. As long as Grandmother was president, a matter of two years, they got it. Later Dad became president of what was then the largest miners' union in the United States. There were 1100 members.

Uncle Robert was alderman of the Second Ward. Uncle George had been town constable for twenty years. Pete Thompson and Will Bolden, businessmen of color, offered competition to the company stores downtown. Ed Owens, a mulatto, was one of the few mail carriers. Aunt Ida was receptionist and nurse in the offices of Dr. Gillis, reputed to be the best surgeon in southern Illinois. Uncle Lewis, who worked at the Elk's Club, held in his saffron hands a hundred skeletons from the closets of the town's elite.

Nor was there any need to try to shame us with red-eyed Eli Gregory, who drank up Aunt Gabe's wash money as

228

fast as she made it. Eli's companions in crime were two nondescript white characters known only as Pony and Sally. If Julia Peterkin's story of *Scarlet Sister Mary* had reached our ears, we would have shrugged and pointed to Queenie Roudy, a mixture of Scotch-Irish and German. Her fifteen children never knew any man as father. The birth of her last baby was attended by her oldest boy, Will, who sat by the bed holding Queenie's hand.

"It's a-comin', Ma, it's a comin'." Will encouraged Queenie in a sing-song voice. "Jes' keep bearin' down, Ma. Jes' keep a-bearin' down."

Just as no one thought of lynching Eli Gregory because he and Sally drank beer from the same bottle, people showed no surprise when Nicholi Bonelli, Italian tenor, selected Wesley Turner, our cousin, with his brown singing hands, to be his accompanist. Nicholi would come down to Wesley's house and for hours the Bottoms would ring with the silvery passages of "O Sole Mio," "Santa Lucia," "La Donna e Mobile," "Veste la Guba," and other classics. They were accepted in the best homes, and a program with their names on it meant a sold-out house. Nicholi begged Wesley to quit the mines and go on tour with him, but Wesley was shy and couldn't pull himself away from his willing entombment.

Du Quoin's great inconsistency was the segregated school system that housed all Negro students in the Lincoln School. In our young minds there was no stigma attached to this procedure for the school building was as nice as any in town, and what was lacking in equipment and playground space was compensated for by the personal interest the Negro teachers took in us and the many extra-curricular affairs planned without the knowledge or approval of the superintendent or the school board.

In this one thing Dad felt defeated, for not only did the teachers think that he wanted their jobs for some special friend of his, but many of the Negroes thought Dad had a personal spite against the teachers. Dad was a flea in the school board's sock. He pestered them every meeting until they finally told him that Helen and I could go to Township High. "No, thank you," Dad snapped. Lacking the backing of his people on this issue, Dad snorted, "They cain't see no farther than their noses," and wrote the school situation off as a bad debt.

Like the school situation, there were other blind spots in our pattern of democratic living and we were completely unprepared for the news our cousin, Raymond Thompson, brought one evening just about suppertime. Raymond was Aunt Judith and Uncle Charlie Thompson's second boy. He was always polite, but this afternoon there was an excitement that overlaid his usual composure. He greeted us warmly. We broke up the ring game we were playing and followed him into the house.

"Aunt Sophia," he addressed Mother in somewhat the same manner a military scout reports "mission completed," "I'm going to work at Park's Drug Store."

"That's fine, Raymond." Mother's praise was warm, yet rather casual. She sounded as though it were the custom to employ black boys behind the counter of the biggest white drugstore in our town.

Most boys of Raymond's age were thinking about quitting school and getting a job in the mines, or at Will Hayes' soft drink plant and icehouse. Certainly, if they continued in school they worked as trap or pit boys in the mines during summer, or served their apprenticeship as coal diggers under the watchful supervision of a father or uncle. Such opportunity was denied Raymond, for his father did not work in the mines. He was a paper hanger who was also the leading basso profundo in the Mount Zion Baptist Church choir.

"Charlie charges you for papering and throws in the concert free." Mother would smile as she thought of Uncle Charlie at work. His repertoire was limited but he made up in vigor what he lacked in variety. If he worked for you half a day you were sure to hear, over and over again, "The Sentinel Asleep," "Absent," "Asleep in the Deep," and "The Big Bass Viol."

Helen had reached the age of hero worship. Maurice Costello was her matinee idol. Now here was our own cousin to be employed at Park's Drug Store. Negro clerks were by no means new to Du Quoin, but they were scattered in neighborhoods predominantly Negroid. Raymond, according to his story, was to begin clerking in the nicest, largest drugstore on Main Street.

"Gee!" Helen was thrilled. "That's wonderful!"

"What you gonna be doing?" Spud wanted to know.

"I'm going to wait on customers."

"On everybody?" I asked. Willie Jackson worked in Arthur Angel's Drug Store, but he didn't do much waiting on people. He did a lot of sweeping and scrubbing and opening cardboard boxes.

"Sure," Raymond answered. "Why not? Mr. Parks says he's going to teach Mike Bianco and me the business."

"That's wonderful, Raymond. I'm glad to see you aspire for a profession. Not that mining isn't honorable. It is," Mother defended, "but we need to advance. I'm glad for Mike, too. He's a fine boy."

Raymond didn't stay long. Seeing that we were duly impressed, he started back up the street. It seemed that he had added two inches to his short stature.

Good news tells itself, or how else did Dad and the other miners know about Raymond and Mike before they reached our house. We could hear them plainly as they stood talking by Ernest Smith's gate.

"It's a mighty fine thing," Dad commented.

"A damn fine thing, if it's true," Pat Holden agreed.

"That Thompson boy will make good."

"Wat Parks knows a man when he sees one."

"Nice of him to give that Eye-talian boy a chance, too."

"Damn nice," Dominic nodded his head. "Me an' Mike's old man come to America on-a da same boat—fourth class—steerage—all-a da way. Maybe Joe Bianco's boy will be da rich man some day. Damn nice country—dis America. Damn nice people."

"Sure," Frank Molsen from Poland agreed, "dots vy Frieda an' me bring da kids from da ole country. Us"—he shrugged his shoulders—"we no matter. But Charlie, Anna, and little Yeets. They must go up—up." He spiraled his hand to give emphasis to his words. "I don't want da boys should crawl around under da ground like a Goddamned mole."

The men were silent for a time. As soon as Frank Molsen, Dominic, and Pat Holden went up the street, Cecil and I sprinted across the road.

"Leave anything in your bucket, Dad?" we yelled as we raced toward him.

"Divide it even," Dad admonished as he gave us his lunch pail. We yanked off the lid. A lone Roman Beauty apple rolled about the till. Things always tasted better when Dad brought them back from the mines.

"Break it for us, Dad." I gave the big apple to my father. He pressed his thumbs hard where the apple joined the short stem, then taking each side between his strong hands, he broke the apple in half, gave each of us our share and continued his conversation with the men. Ernest Smith, Willie, Wesley and Babe Turner, Miles Lane, and Charlie Fox stood looking up the street without actually being aware of the houses or the dirt road.

"Raymond will end up with a broom or a mop and bucket," Charlie Fox spoke with bitterness. Charlie Fox didn't like white people. There was some talk that he had escaped from a chain gang down south, but nobody seemed to know for sure.

"I don't know," Ernest Smith said thoughtfully.

"Well, I know!" Dad was positive. "Whatever Wat Parks told him, he can bet his bottom dollar on that. Now if he was dependin' on Ole Man Beesman, I wouldn't trust him no further than I could throw him. Beesman'd tell a lie on credit when he could get cash for the truth—an' he wouldn't give the Lord a prayer. But Wat is different. He's like his daddy before him. A man's a man with Wat Parks. He don't judge a man by the color of his skin."

"Well, what's he gonna get out of it?" Babe wanted to know.

"Maybe he's gonna run for some office next election. He knows he can't win without the colored and Italian vote." Ernest was practical.

"I keep trying to tell you Wat Parks ain't that kind of man," Dad defended.

"We'll see—when election time comes." Dad had not convinced Ernest.

" 'Course I can see him hirin' Mike Bianco," Willie reasoned.

"Raymond's more American than Mike. You just heard Dominic say Mike's old man came over with him from

Italy. Raymond's folks have been here since God-knows-when," Wesley retorted.

"Yes, but Mike's got the difference," Miles Lane said slowly.

"What difference?" Dad and Wesley wanted to know.

"If he's white—he's all right. Brown? He can sorta stick around; but if he's black—he must stay back," Miles droned.

"You talk like a fool, man. A addle-brained, hatchet-faced fool!" Dad thundered. "A black man don't have to stand back for nobody. We don't in the mines. In the union a black vote is as good as a white one. Don't white folks come to us on their hands and knees at election time begging for our votes?"

"The head must bow and the back will have to bend, wherever the darky may go," Willie Turner sang softly.

"That's another lie," Dad shouted. "Where'd that come from?"

"That's what your children sing in school. It's in their song books——" Willie began.

Dad whirled swiftly. His hard, calloused hands gripped our shoulders. "Ruby, you and Cecil listen to me. Do you sing that song in school?"

"Sometimes. It's 'My Old Kentucky Home.'" Usually Mr. Barnett tells us to skip that verse," I answered.

"And I used to like that song. I thought it was a good song. Lis'en, don't you never sing that verse, not as lon' as God keeps makin' little apples. If the teacher ask you why you don't sing, tell 'im I tole you not to. He can't make you sing it and he better not lay the weight of his finger on you. Not unless he wants to shake hands with Jesus." His hard grip loosened on our shoulders. We smiled at him, then at each other.

"You don't never have to sing that verse—no siree, not

as long as heaven's happy," Dad repeated. And we knew that was the word with the bark on it. "I never have seen a man that I thought was better than me. I've seen 'em who had more money, sure; or more book learnin', but that don't make him better inside, not by a long shot."

"Ain't no need of us arguing among ourselves," Wesley, the peacemaker reasoned. "One thing is sure—time will tell."

The next day we had business by Park's Drug Store. Sure enough, there was Raymond behind a shining glass show-case filled with oddly-shaped perfume bottles. Lillian Dreuer, the town belle and an aspiring concert pianist, was leaning over the counter as Raymond waved the stopper of a bottle under her freckled stubbed nose.

"Um-m-m," she breathed. "That's heavenly. What's it called, Raymond?"

"It's new. Mrs. Parks says it's the nicest perfume we have. It just came in yesterday. It is called Black Narcissus."

We looked about the store. We didn't see any evidence of Raymond's broom or mop. Raymond was dressed in a nicely pressed blue serge suit. He wore a white shirt with a stiff detachable collar. A knitted four-in-hand tie was tucked neatly into his vest. Maybe Mike Bianco was doing the sweeping. But even as we thought it, Mike came smiling from the rear of the store. He was dressed in a pair of light-colored trousers and a woolen pull-on sweater.

Mary and Pete Fantaco had brought several other Italian children into the store by this time. Now Mrs. Parks came from behind the partition. She spoke to Lillian Druer and started across the store to wait on us.

"Mrs. Parks," Raymond spoke to her, "you know more about this than I do. Would you mind helping Lillian? I think I can take care of the kids."

"Of course not, Raymond." Mrs. Parks took the scent bottle from Raymond's hand.

Now Raymond and Mike stood behind the same counter. They smiled at each other as though they were enjoying a huge joke.

"And what is it for you?" Mike greeted the Fantaco children pleasantly.

"Two raspberry suckers." Mary dropped two pennies on the counter. They backed out the door looking first at Mike, then at Raymond. They hadn't even started to take the wrappers off the candy.

"Can I help you?" There was a new sparkle in Raymond's eyes as he smiled at us.

"We want a pineapple sucker, a licorice jawbreaker, and a two-cent stamp."

"My, my, where did you get all that money?" Raymond teased.

"Aunt Ida gave us the two pennies for going on an errand for her. Mama's buying the stamp. She's writing to Aunt Della Hayden in Jackson, Mississippi."

"Tell her to remember me to Aunt Della."

"We will." We started for the door. "Bye Raymond."

"Bye. Thanks and call again."

Once out the door nothing detained us. We didn't even pause to sniff the freshly baked bread as we passed Geiger's Bakery. The cooperage and Frog Larson failed to halt our steps. We heard the sound of his hammer and one line of his weary blues, "Mah baby she quit me an' done gone——"

We were the harbingers of a great event. It had happened, even as Raymond had said. A slave's grandson and the son of an Italian immigrant were waiting on customers in the nicest, biggest drugstore in our town.

24. *the ugly mask of fear*

The night started out to be one of those normal cold winter nights that found Dad sitting by the big base-burner in his stocking feet, with his top shirt off and his red and blue suspenders making a colorful pattern against his ecru woolen undershirt. He was reading the Du Quoin *Evening Call*. Mother sat on the other side of the stove with a basket of overalls to be mended. She was sewing down the patch on the knee of the pair she had in her lap.

Trying to understand Harold Bell Wright's *Uncrowned King*, I was dimly aware of Spud and Tom playing on the other side of the room. Spud was being Spartacus, king of the Greek gladiators, and the sawed-off mop that he was using as his sword made murderous sounds that mixed up with Tom's squeals of delight. Cecil was having trouble with long division.

Helen, who had been busy parching field corn in an iron skillet, now came from the kitchen with Bob and Cliff at her heels. She carried an earthen crock filled with the brown grains seasoned with salt and butter.

The cause of the gladiators was forgotten as small brown hands reached eagerly into the bowl for the crisp grains.

The moaning and crying of the searching wind outside only added to our sense of security and well-being. The heat from the round-bellied stove sent its warmth into the

237

farthest corner of the room and we were settled contentedly and gratefully for the night.

"Wild horses couldn't drag me out on a night like this." Dad spoke for us all as he rose, stretched himself, and laid the paper on the table. Dad had reckoned without fate.

The hammering at the door was loud and insistent.

Hurrying to the door, Dad threw it open and Derby George, a cousin, Uncle Robert Berkley, and their friend, Ottoway Scott, followed a blast of cold wind into the room.

For a second Dad's "Good evening, gentlemen," went unanswered by the three men who stood just inside the door, their overcoat collars turned up around their necks and tightly buttoned against the wind. The bills of their fleece-lined caps were pulled down over their foreheads but the eyes that peered from beneath them were filled with urgency and grave concern.

"You gotta come with us, Buddy," Uncle Robert said without preliminaries. "J. T. Perkins has killed a white man!"

I made myself small as did all the children when grown-up tragedy broke into our happy world and a terror came over me. Instinctively Bob and Cliff, who had been following Helen about the room, crowded close to Mother. Spud and Tom sat hunched on the floor, eyes fixed on Dad and the three men, and they waited as I waited, for the word that would send us from the room. But the word was never spoken. Our presence was completely forgotten.

I heard Dad ask quietly if J. T. Perkins was "the scary-looking little fella" who had been "made" at the Odd Fellows last meeting, and I saw Ottoway Scott try to speak, then change his mind and nod heavily.

There was something in this that I could not understand. Mother stood with her arms crossed over her breasts, as

238

though the doors had suddenly opened all through the house and the wind was howling and tearing at us.

As Dad stuffed his shirttail into his trousers, she hurried into the bedroom and returned with his woolen sweater and overcoat. The men had not taken the offered chairs, but stood impatiently and glanced furtively toward the windows. Spud now looked at Dad. A hundred unanswered questions shone from the depths of his dark brown eyes. He opened his mouth, but I nudged him with my foot and slowly shook my head as he glanced toward me.

Hurried good nights were said, and Dad followed the men out into the darkness. I went to the east window to lower the shade. Dad, Uncle Robert, Derby George, and Ottoway Scott had crossed the street and were passing the gaslight that stood between Uncle George's house and the Sadberry place. The men were bent forward in the cold wind and their overcoats billowed out like small tepees.

The closing of the door galvanized us into action. The smaller children pulled at Mother's skirts. There was a question on everybody's lips. Mother tenderly disengaged chubby fists and greasy hands and in her quiet, patient way said, "You know as much as I know. It's way past your bedtime. We'll know everything when your father comes home." Ashy brown legs stuck out from beneath the tails of flannelette nightshirts as the boys knelt at Mother's knee and repeated, "Now I lay me down to sleep——" Mother followed them into the room, tucked them in bed and returned to her basket of mending. Her face above the mending had lost its calmness. Her features were drawn and tired.

It was well after midnight when Dad returned. He was not alone. The house was in darkness save for the tiny glow from the coal oil lamp in the kitchen that had been turned down very low. Helen and I were asleep on the folding bed in the living room. I cannot tell what awakened me. I heard the click of the night latch and the scraping of feet on the front steps. Again a cold draft of air circled the room.

"Wait 'til I get a light from the other room," I heard Dad say in a low voice. He was soon back, had placed the lamp on the small table, and was adjusting the wick.

"I'll stir up the fire a bit." The tops had been cut out of two powder kegs. Holes had been drilled in the sides and bailing wire run through to make the handles. These were our coal buckets and they sat filled behind the base-burner. Dad poked into the stove with a long iron poker, turning up the red-hot coals. He turned the damper in the stove-pipe. With his hands he scooped up the small pieces of nut coal, then added a larger chunk.

I did not see the man Dad had brought to the house until he moved away from the door and now stood warming himself by the fire. Instinctively I knew this was J. T. Perkins, but Dad's description was a gross understatement. "Sort of a scary-looking little fella" didn't tell half the terror that showed itself in the beady black eyes. There was a hesitancy about his every move, and you felt that he always met life by running away from it.

He sat on the edge of the chair Dad had placed for him. As he watched Dad move about the room, you sensed a pleading that wanted to make itself heard above the fear.

"I guess I shoulda went on over to Mr. Robert and Miss Sally's house with him, but I wanted to talk to you alone. I'm glad Miss Sally took Emma and the children with her— but—I don't want no harm to come to them or you either on account of what I done tonight."

"On account of what you done? Harm come to us?" Dad couldn't quite make the connection.

"You know that big policeman was gonna take me to jail before you got there."

"Well, that's what he's getting paid for, and he didn't know you." Dad never called a spade a shovel. "Charlie Layman knows I'm a man of my word and if I told him I'd stand good for you—— Well, that's good enough for him."

"I know what I'm in for. Maybe it woulda happened tonight if I'da been in jail. Sposen they come looking for me."

"Looking for you for what? You'll get your hearing when Judge Cook opens court tomorrow."

"Looks like the Lord don't aim for me to know no peace."

"Folks blame too many things on the Lord. He didn't have nothing to do with what happened tonight. It's the cussedness of men what causes all the trouble."

"Maybe you're right," J. T. admitted doubtfully.

"'Course I'm right." Dad agreed with him.

"At any rate, you got a right to know why I come to Du Quoin. I didn't know this town was on the face of God's green earth. We worked a piece of land in Mississippi, Mr. Berkley. Me and my brother farmed side by side. We worked hard. God knows we did. Every year the boss would say, 'J. T., you nearly come out even. You owe jes' a little bit but I'll stake you next year.' My brother Ed got discouraged. He started making the children teach him to figure like they was learning at school."

"Then one year my brother walked up to the boss with a gang of figures."

" 'Boss man, you done cheated me for the las' time,' Ed told him."

"The boss man looked at the figures and laughed. Then he started tearing the paper into little bits. My brother reached to take the papers outa his hands—and he shot 'im dead. Said my brother Ed was trying to hit him. That night they come and burned our houses down. Some friends hid us for two or three days. They took up some money. This was as far north as the money would send us. They killed my brother for nothin', Mr. Berkley. He ain't done a God's thing. Now what you think they gonna do to me? I killed a white man, see? I *killed a white man!*"

"You couldn't help it. Nobody ain't gonna hold that agin you. Shucks, it was your house, wasn't it? You'd be less than a man if you didn't protect your home. 'Course, I must say," Dad added, "you wasn't particular where you took your wife an' children."

"I couldn't pick my place. I landed in Du Quoin with seven dollars. The house wasn't nothing but a shack but the man let us have it for five dollars a month."

"He didn't tell you who'd lived in that house before you came?"

"I didn't ask him. It was snowing when we got here. I was glad to get a roof over the children's heads. I knowed what was going on around me. Two or three times fellas had said something to Emma. None of 'em tried to get rough and one even apologized when he saw little Mattie hanging on her ma's skirts. But this 'un tonight was different." Perkins' voice was low, but you were conscious of the screaming underneath that he kept back by a superhuman strength he had summoned from outside his weak spirit.

"We heard the fella come upon the porch. He banged

on the door and started cussing when nobody opened it for him. We didn't want to wake up the children. You're at the wrong house, I said kinda soft like. That settled it. I ain't never heard such talk."

"Who you got in there, you two-timing, double-crossing bitch. You better open this Goddamned door or I'll break it off its hinges!"

"The children woke up and run over to me and their mother. They was still scared from the burning and the hiding. They didn't cry out loud; they jes' tried to get under the cover and they made little whimpering noises like a hound dog after he's had a good beatin' for stealin' eggs."

"You gotta do somethin', J. T.," Emma pleaded. "Pore little things are scared to death."

"I remembered an ole rabbit gun I brought with me. Honest to God, Mr. Berkley, I ain't never thought of killin' a man in my life. I crept out of bed and got the gun. Even then I warned him:

" 'Get away from that door,' I said loud this time. 'Get away from that door or I'll shoot.'

"His laff was ugly and hard."

" 'Wait 'til I get my hands on you, you Goddamned son of a bitch.' He lunged against the door and I musta pulled the trigger. The gun went off and the wood in the door seemed to be ripped apart. Then something heavy hit the porch. I never heard nothing but a low moan. Finally I went over to the door, unlocked it, and looked out."

All the while J. T. had been talking he was staring straight at the isinglass in the door of the stove. Now he covered his face with his hands and his body trembled. Whether remorse was stronger than fear I cannot say, for both were in his voice. He had slid from the chair and was groveling on the floor on his hands and knees.

Dad put a reassuring hand on his arm and pulled him to his feet. The strong lines in Dad's face were softened by pity. His voice was kind but stern, and I recalled the day he talked to us as he battered the head of a large water moccasin that had frightened us as we were crossing the little creek that ran through our land.

"What's done's done, man. Ain't no need of cutting yourself to pieces talkin' about it."

"He never moved. He never moved," J. T. kept repeating. "He just laid there staring straight up at the roof of the porch. A pint of whiskey fell outa his pocket and was laying there beside him. You don't seem to understand, Mr. Berkley—I done killed a white man!"

"I know, but that ain't no worse than killing any other kind o' man. They're all the same, two hands, two feet, two eyes, two ears, and an itch for a woman. Thas why he was at your house. Get me straight. It's wrong to kill any human being, black or white. It's wrong 'cause you're taking life an' thas something that you cain't give. But color ain't got nothing to do with it."

"Black folks ain't nothing nohow; ain't born for nothin' but trouble."

"You jes' talkin' fool talk now. Black folks got a whole lot to give the world as soon as the world get sense enough to know it. Black men done taught 'em a lot anyhow. Solomon was the wisest man what ever lived. He founded the Masonic Lodge and he said hisself that he was black. They tell me the first American to die in the Revolutionary War was a black man named Crispus Something or ruther."

"Sho nuff, Mr. Berkley?"

"Sho-er than that. Now you go on over to Robert's and get some sleep. You ain't got no cause to be worried. Nobody ain't gonna bother you tonight, and Judge Cook is as fair a man as ever wore britches."

"You got a powerful strong arm for folks to lean on, Mr. Berkley. Thank you, thank you kindly."

"I'll walk with you over to Robert's. It's just a little way an' I ain't sleepy." Dad threw his overcoat about his shoulders and followed J. T. out into the darkness.

When he returned, he sat by the fire for a long time.

"Better come to bed, Braxton," Mother called softly.

Dad tilted the damper on the stovepipe, turned the lamp wick down, and blew out the light. I heard his slow steps. The sagging springs creaked and groaned as he eased his weight down upon the old walnut bed with the high headboard.

I do not know how long I lay awake. I had become aware of the world beyond the peace and security I had known. This new world was a strange and ugly place in which to live. It was a world where a man could be shot dead because he dared to ask for an accounting of his wages. It was a world where a man's house could be burned to the ground and some men in high places would never ask questions.

Suddenly the world became peopled with frightened, weak people, terribly confused people. But somehow, above the horror of the picture I saw my dad, big, strong, bronzed Braxton Berkley, holding back the world and shielding his children and those he loved.

I went to sleep with the words of J. T. Perkins filling the friendly darkness of the quiet room, "You got a powerful strong arm for folks to lean on, Mr. Berkley."

25. black and powerful

Every school day was an exciting chapter in the romance of learning—but not so today. I was weighted down by an inertia that was filled with foreboding. My mind refused to travel again the horror-strewn path of last night, but I could not go around it or rise above it. I could not explain the physical fatigue that seemed to keep my body pinned to the bed long after Mother had called us. I only knew that I needed the security of the four walls of our home. I wanted to hear the satisfying sound of my father's voice. I needed the quiet strength of my mother as she moved about the house doing the many always-to-be-done things.

Spud, Cecil, and Helen dressed hurriedly for school. Their short questions concerning the happening of the night before were answered curtly by Mother's "We'll have to wait and find out." I scarcely touched my breakfast. Gathering up my books, I slowly followed them out into the street.

There was no work that morning and the men left their homes to gather downtown. Brave men walk alone but the fearful need the security of the pack; so each called to his neighbor, or waited for him at the corner. The air was cold and crisp and the warm vapor from the men's nostrils hung in the air like fragile wreaths of cigarette smoke.

The women called to each other as they threw chopped

corn to their chickens or drew water from their boxed-in wells.

Mary Stevenson, her face nearly hidden in the brightly colored homespun shawl she had brought from the highlands of Scotland, shook her head sorrowfully as she unconsciously patted the shoulder of the bonnie lad that clung to her skirts. " 'Tis said the poor man cried like a bleatin' sheep when he knew he had killed 'im."

"Ya, ya," Maria Chlefek nodded her head vigorously.

Mariah Winston had stopped Cousin Frankie as the latter felt her way across the road. "I done prayed, Frankie, I tell you I done prayed, an' like Daniel, J. T. Perkins gonna walk through the fire an' ain't even gonna get singed. God is above the devil evva day."

Cousin Frankie, whose supplication for sight had gone unrewarded for many years was not so emphatic as she answered, "I hope you're right, Mariah, I hope you're right. I know I been prayin' evva since I heard about it."

At school, we did not loiter outside to play. The weather was much too cold. We hurried into the brown-glazed brick building and on to our rooms. There was no good-natured jostling of each other in the halls, no enthusiastic biting of each other's apples, or nibbling the ends of peppermint sticks. Sensing the weight of the tragedy that had blanketed the town, we moved slowly and quietly to our seats. Mrs. Anderson, Emma Tate, and William Barnett who whispered to each other in the hall, became silent, as though by mutual consent, when we came within listening distance.

All morning long I had assumed an indifference I did not feel. As much as I wanted to, I could not share the complete story with Spud, for it was not mine to share. It was J. T.

Perkins' secret and he had been careful, even in his fear, not to tell it to anyone except Dad. Spud had tried to talk to me about the killing, but I was strangely noncommittal. Finally he excused me by saying, "Ain't fellin' well—or something, Ruby?"

It was noon before we knew what had really happened at the inquest. We were almost home when we saw Simon leaving the gasworks. I wanted to ask if he had heard anything, but was afraid. It was Spud who spoke up as Simon approached us. "Heard anything about Mr. Perkins yet, Simon?"

"Sho, Spud, sho. The coroner's jury done let him go scot free." Simon pulled out his watch, held it at arm's length, and announced with dramatic severity, "He been free well nigh onto two hours. They said it was justifiable home-inside."

Farther down the street Mariah Winston, like a good soldier of the cross, marched with banners flying. She lifted her voice like a trumpet and though she was only addressing herself to Cousin Frankie and Aunt Nettie, she could be heard all over the Bottoms.

"Well, glory!" she shouted, as she paused for a little while before their door. Her raised right arm quivered above her head. Tears of joy glistened on her brown cheeks and dropped unheeded on the hard-packed snow at her feet. "I tole you this mawnin', Frankie, that God is above the devil. Thas why I holds onto him. Like pepper an' salt in country sausage, I'm rooted an' grounded, twisted an' tied in the Lord Jesus, an' you can tell ole Satan I ain't bothered!"

Dinner was on the table when we entered the house, but I was not hungry. I passed through the living room and lay down on Mother's bed. There was something about Moth-

er's bed that had a curative effect on us whether the ill was
of the body or of the spirit. Mother came into the room.
She was never given to superfluous talk. Taking a blanket
from the quilt box behind the door, she spread it over me
and returned to the kitchen.

I was vaguely conscious of the rattle of dishes as they were
being piled with the knives and forks on the small table to
be washed. Chairs were pushed noisily aside. Spud's voice
sounded in the doorway as he called, "Ruby." I raised my
head to answer, but Mother interrupted with a "don't
bother her. She can miss one afternoon."

A chorus of "bye," preceded the closing of the outer door
and the metallic click of the night latch.

A quietness descended upon the house. The drone of
voices in the kitchen seemed to dissolve into it. Dad's voice
came from a long way off.

"Jes' like you know the runt pig gonna outweigh all the
rest of the brood, you know the spirit of each child God
gives you." For a few seconds there was complete silence,
then the voice continued, "She's gonna be the deep thinkin'
one—the deep feelin' one."

"Wish she was more like Helen. Helen's going to wear
this world as a loose garment," Mother commented in a
higher-pitched voice.

"She ain't gonna be content to carry her own load. She'll
try to be a burden bearer for other folks an' it's a hard an'
thankless job," Dad's voice sounded weary.

"You ought to know," Mother agreed.

Lying there on the bed I felt detached and alone—out of
touch with the world I knew and loved. That a man I
scarcely knew had the power to do this to my hitherto
secure world frightened me. J. T. Perkins was free, yet I

felt chained by the things I had witnessed through his frightened eyes. I tried to search back through my childhood to find something that would help me understand the people who had burned J. T. Perkins' home, the man who had shot his brother.

I vaguely sensed that I had met this terror before. Painted and masked to hide its frightfulness but there just the same. It was all bound up in my being called "Topsy," in Maggie Daniels casual remark concerning an explosion, " 'Twasn't bad, just killed twenty mules and a nigger." Too, I remembered the day when Willie had laughingly repeated a line of a Stephen Foster song, "The head must bow and the back will have to bend, wherever the darky may go." Dad's anger had seemed all out of proportion to the words of the simple song, yet instinctively I felt that each had its place in the ugly picture that appeared before me.

Was this the world that I would meet as soon as I went beyond the borders of my own town? Or even in the confines of my friendly birthplace; could something happen that would make our neighbors a pack of howling strangers, crying for blood?

I do not know when the tears came. I was conscious of a small trickle that scurried across the bridge of my nose and down my cheek to be soaked up by the pillow. I did not want to cry. Crying was a sign of weakness and was the first line of defense for girls and women. I had always scorned tears, but now they came—at first slowly and noiselessly as the first light drops of an April shower. Then came the deluge when they gushed from tightly closed lids to form a damp ring on the pillowcase. I caught my breath in an effort to hold back the sobs that welled up in my throat.

I felt the soft touch of a hand on my head. I tried to stop

the tears but they only came the faster. I pulled the blanket up to my eyes and turned my face to the wall. Two gentle but firm hands raised me. Dad eased himself down on the side of the bed and cradled my head in his arms.

For a time only the short irregular intakes of breath disturbed the silence. I wiped my eyes with the blue and white kerchief Dad had stuffed into my tightly closed fist. I tried to control the jerking of taut muscles, but he seemed to understand and only held me closer.

"I'm sorry you had to know about these things, Reuben," he stated simply with no preliminary remarks. "I'd give my right arm to shield you from some of the things you're gonna have to face. I ain't scared for your courage. You got plenty of that. But every father wants a smooth path for his children's feet an' I cain't guarantee you that. Maybe I shoulda tole you a long time ago about some of the things you gonna be learnin' from now on, but I 'llowed I'd stand between my children an' the gun as long as I could.

"Maybe I didn't tell you because I didn't know jus' where to begin. You heard J. T. Perkins talking to me last night." Dad did not ask a question, he merely sought confirmation for what he seemed to know was the truth. I nodded my head and felt the soft scratching of the brown woolen shirt against my cheek.

"Perkins said a lot of things las' night. Some of 'em was true, then some you'll have to take with a grain of salt. Perkins was scared and when a man's scared he'll say anything. He'll blame everything but his own weakness. You'll find plenty folks runnin' 'round scared. Some of 'em are scared of their own shadows. Then," he reflected, "some things ain't shadows, but you cain't whup nothin' runnin' away from it. You got to meet trouble if you want to land a good lick.

"You heard Perkins say black folks ain't nothin'. Thas fool talk. Black ain't nothin' to be ashamed of. Some people thinks it's dirt under their feet or a pile o' chicken manure in the back lot. I'm proud when somebody calls me a black man. Black has strength and"—I could feel the swell of his broad chest beneath the brown wool as he added one word more—"dignity. The Bible says God made man out of the dust of the earth. I've seen red dirt, brown dirt, black dirt, and yellow clay, but all my life I ain't never seen no real white dirt.

"We ain't got many real black men." I shifted my head and looked up at Dad strangely. "White men done seen to that," was all the explanation he offered.

"I look at some of our folks. They want to be white so bad they can taste it. They think 'cause they're light brown or yellow, they're better than dark people. They ain't. They ain't as good. We're the only people I know who are proud of being bast—well, someday when you're a little bigger you'll understand.

"We ought to be proud of being black, Reuben. Black is powerful. You can take it anyway you want to. If the world knows a race of supermen, it's the black folks in America. Someday you'll learn these things from your books in school. I never had much schoolin'. When I shoulda been goin' to the fourth grade I was diggin' as much coal as a man at Ole Enterprise mines, but I listened to the ole folks talk. They knowed a heap."

Through Dad's eyes, the awful cavalcade of human slavery marched before me. I saw men and women who had only known the freedom of the jungle and the veldt, bound and shackled, being driven like beasts through strange country until they reached the seacoast. The stench of the slave ship invaded the room as Dad described the human cargo stacked like cordwood in the hold of the vessel. His speaking was divided by uneven silences. Sometimes his voice was so low it seemed that he was talking more to himself than to me.

"Slavery wasn't no bed of roses neither," he continued after a while. "My father run off three times before he was set free. Every time he was caught an' sold again. He was never caught by his own master, but any white man could catch him an' sell him—because a slave didn't have no rights.

"Yes, slavery was a terrible thing, but the black man was able to rise above the beatin's and the sellin's an' the awfulness of the time. He never los' hope, an' a man is never whupped if he has hope. They worked 'em like mules, they beat 'em like dogs, but the hope wouldn't die. It growed like a blade of grass stickin' up through a crack in a rock.

"Freedom wasn't all it was cracked up to be neither. For 300 years a whole nation of people had been told what to do, where to go, an' when to come. Now, jes' like that," Dad snapped his fingers, "they was turned loose an' told to root hog, or die. You got your freedom, nigger, now what you gonna do with it?

"The black man looked around. Folks eyein' him like a cow lookin' at las' year's calf. Everybody gotta have someone to look down on, I guess. Makes 'em feel big an' important. But always remember, it don't matter how much other people look down on you as long as you don't look down on yourself.

"Jes' look at what yore Grandpa Berkley done, chile. At

one time he owned almost as much lan' as Ole Man Lipe, and Ole Man Lipe been free all his life. I can remember when I was jes' a strip of a boy. Dad had cans of money settin' on the pantry shelves behind the groceries. He put some of it in the bank too, but he used to say to me, 'Braxton, you cain't let the white fo'ks know all yore business.' Len Berkley was a smart ole man. Smart an' black an' powerful. The only other man I ever knowed who was stronger than Dad was Rich Burdett. Everybody called him Blue. Rich was so black a piece o' coal would make a chalk mark on him. One day I saw him lift the hind end of a car of coal off Al Hickman at Forester's mines.

"Some fo'ks say they pity black people. We don't need pity. All we need is a chance. We know how to work an' we know how to have fun. Tha's more than mos' white fo'ks know. Each one of 'em have to be the bell cow or he won't gallop with the gang. We work hard, but in the evenin' what do we do? If there's a meetin', we go to that; if there ain't, we might go up an' chew the fat with some of the boys in front of John Simmon's pool hall, but we'd jes' as soon stay home an' play ball, or play run, sheep, run, or tell stories to you children that the ole fo'ks used to tell us.

"Sometimes we jes' feel like singin', so we all gang up on Ida's porch. Dea builds a smoke at one end to keep the mosquitoes away—an' we sing. None of us never had a lesson, but that don't bother us none. It would bother some white fo'ks 'cause everything they do they got to think about it an' worry over it. White fo'ks sing from the head. Black man sings from the heart, an' when a group of us get together it sounds like the angels singin' 'round the throne of God."

For a long time Dad was silent. "Dad." I nudged him gently. "Dad, wouldn't it be nice to live in a town where there were nothing but colored people?"

"You been listenin' to that ole pot-gutted fool that stayed over to Belle's house. He come up here tryin' to get colored people to go to some little ole pig path in Arkansas to start up a town. Naw, Ruby, a handful of Negroes stuck off in a little corner by themselves ain't the answer. Sometimes a fellow leans over backwards trying to make his point. I been trying to tell you that you ain't got no cause to be ashamed of being black. Some black fo'ks are the best in the world. Then some of 'em are regular tush hogs. There's some good white fo'ks, too, Reuben. Never forget that. If all the white people was mean an' low down, a pore colored man wouldn't stand a chance. It's all right to have a fightin' heart, but you cain't whup the world with yore bare hands. God didn't make no mistake when he made all kinds an' colors of people, but he didn't make no race to be master. He didn't make no race to be slaves.

"You'll hear people say the black man's got a strong back an' a weak mind. That's a lie too—a barefaced lie. Solomon was the wisest man the world ever knowed. It says so in the Bible, jes' like I tole J. T. Perkins las' night. Solomon said hisself, 'I am black, but I am comely.'

"Then a black man helped Jesus when he almost give out carryin' his cross up Calvary. That was a great honor an' it was give to a black man. But honor ain't something to stick yore head up in the air about, like Lizzie Fielden when she gets on a new dress. Honor brings along her twin brother, Responsibility. That makes you thoughtful an' kinda humble. Some people mistake being a coward for humility. I don't mean that. Everybody wants to kick a coward in his

255

behind, but there's something about a humble man, there's a sure strength somewhere about him that makes everybody stand off an' look at him. I want you to be proud you're black, Reuben. Black is powerful!"

As I looked into the strong confident face of my dad, I was recharged with a vibrant, pulsing life. The weariness and exhaustion were gone. I was conscious of being hungry and there was the urge to walk out into the cold bright winter afternoon. There was laughter in Dad's eyes as he playfully pushed me back among the pillows, rose from the side of the bed and stretched himself.

"I been runnin' on like an ole woman. Reckon you'd better get up pretty soon. Sophia's got something out in the kitchen that's smellin' powerful good."

I needed no second invitation. Never had cream of tomato soup smelled so good. Maybe it was ambrosia. Why not? After all I was something extra special. J. T. Perkins and his frightened world belonged to the better-to-be-forgotten past. Again I walked the highway of free men where there was nothing to make me afraid. Nothing or nobody had the power to hurt me. I was invincible. It is true I touched hands with the peoples of the world, but even as I touched them, I lifted them with me. I was remembering the potency of black, and suddenly I felt genuinely sorry for everybody in the world lighter than the brown pair of Red Goose shoes laced on my dancing feet.